The Author

Hugh Playfair is a grandson of the Revd Dr Patrick Playfair, Minister of the First Charge of Holy Trinity, St Andrews 1899–1924. He has inherited his grandfather's interests in the Church and churches. Born in St Andrews and brought up in Elie, he was educated at King's College, Cambridge. After National Service in the Somaliland Scouts he became a schoolmaster teaching History in schools in England and Australia. He was baptised into the Church of Scotland and first took part in the Lord's Supper in Holy Trinity Church, St Andrews. In 1987 he was admitted as Reader in the Diocese of Bath and Wells and is currently Chairman of the Diocesan Advisory Committee for the Care of Churches. He was founding Chairman of The Friends of Somerset Churches and Chapels 1995–2005. In 1989 he was appointed OBE for services to the Combined Cadet Force. Married with three children and three grandchildren, he and his wife live in Somerset, but frequently visit St Andrews, the spiritual home of the Playfair family. He is author of *The Playfair Family* and of various pieces about churches, most recently *A Guide to the Churches of Camelot*.

The Town Kirk

Restoration and Ministry
1899–1924

by

Hugh Playfair

Librario

Published by

Librario Publishing Ltd.

ISBN 13: 978-1-906775-02-5

Copies can be ordered via the Internet
www.librario.com

or from:

Brough House, Milton Brodie, Kinloss
Moray IV36 2UA
Tel/Fax No 00 44 (0)1343 850 617

Printed and bound in the UK

Typeset by 3btype.com

*To all who have ministered
and worshipped in this place.*

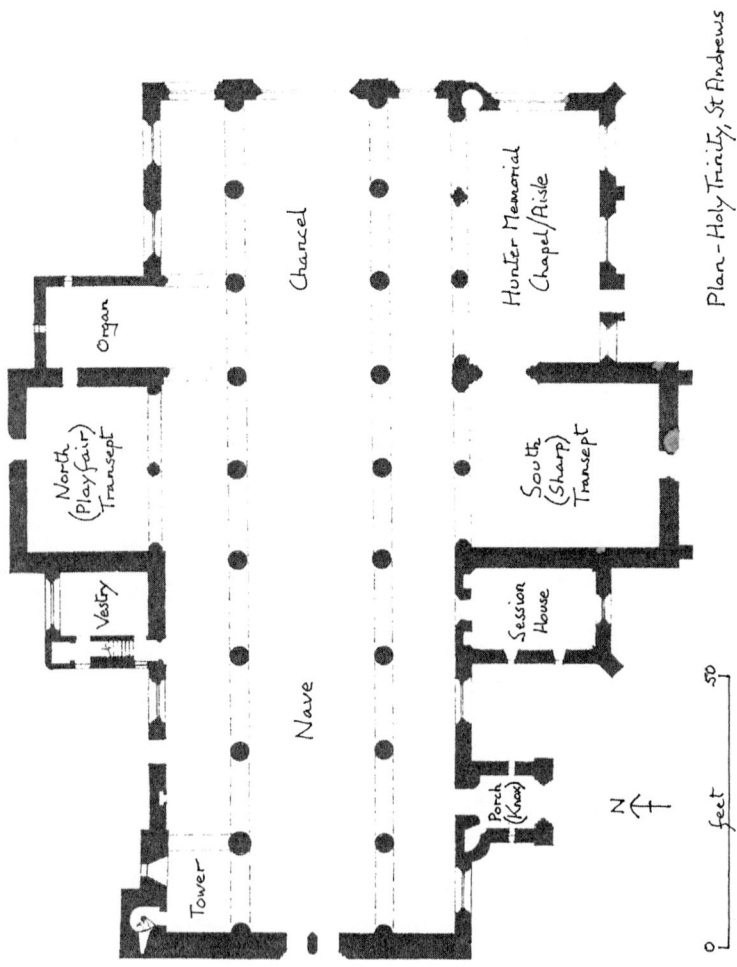

Plan of Holy Trinity Church, St Andrews

6

Introduction

This book commemorates the Centenary of the Rededication of the Church of the Holy Trinity, St Andrews on St Andrew's Day 1909. From that date Holy Trinity or the Town Kirk, as it has been often known, has been closely associated not only with the town of St Andrews but also with the University founded in 1411 and with the game of golf which has been played on the links of St Andrews for over 500 years.

It is essentially the church of the townsfolk and it served as the parish church of the people of St Andrews even before the Reformation in days when the Cathedral flourished. The Archbishop of St Andrews was Rector of Holy Trinity and appointed a Vicar to act as parish priest in his place. Since the Reformation the Minister of Holy Trinity has presided over a church which has played a central role in the life of the town and especially so since the Restoration of 1909. It is the setting for important national as well as municipal occasions such as St Andrew's Day and Remembrance Day services, and services of thanksgiving to remember the lives of deceased sovereigns and victory in war. In days when there was a Town Council the councillors were 'kirked' in Holy Trinity following their election.

There have always been strong links with the University, especially with St Mary's College, though relationships have not always been felicitous. The 500th Anniversary of the Founding of the University was most memorably held in Holy Trinity in 1911. At the time of the Restoration 1906–09 Principal Alexander Stewart and Sir John Herkless, Professor of Ecclesiastical History at St Mary's College were important members of the General and Executive Committees responsible for all aspects of the project. Of course at the time of the Reformation relations were not so cordial, for the University strongly disapproved of the sermons which were being preached from the Town Kirk pulpit.

The connection with the game of golf is also strong. The service each September which celebrates the annual match between the Town and the Royal and Ancient Golf Club is held in Holy Trinity. Tom Morris, who died in 1908 while the work of restoration was in progress, was an esteemed Elder of the Kirk. His life is commemorated by a memorial tablet prominently displayed in the church. There is also a memorial tablet to the legendary American golfer Bobby Jones, a much loved Freeman of the City, whose wife gifted the Bob Jones Bombarde, an extension of the fine organ, in his memory.

All the sermons of my grandfather, Dr Patrick Playfair in this book have been selected and edited, for they are long by the standard and practice of today, from a much larger number of sermons written in his own hand which are now preserved in the St Andrews University Library Department of Special Collections Playfair archive. They are laid out in the order in which they were first preached. All were preached in Holy Trinity though the earlier ones were first preached in his previous parish of Glencairn. Many were subsequently preached in other places for Patrick Playfair was in considerable demand. Two were preached before King George V and Queen Mary at Crathie and five were preached in Rutger's Presbyterian Church, New York, while he was on sabbatical leave. Some of the sermons are of historical interest as they were preached on important occasions, for example on the Sunday morning following the Rededication of Holy Trinity following the Restoration and on the outbreak of World War I. Some of the sermons were preached on important Christian festivals – on Christmas Day and on Easter Sunday. Others examine aspects of Christian doctrine and teaching – the Last Supper, the Trinity, the Miracles of Christ in general and the Feeding of the 5,000 in particular, Christian virtues, and discipleship. Several of the sermons deal with topics of contemporary and abiding interest – love, wisdom, relations between Church and State, faith and doubt, and the countryside. All of them give a definitive and straightforward account of and commentary on essential aspects of the Christian Faith. There is also a children's address on Light.

Preceding the sermons there are three chapters which set the scene. The first chapter is a short biography of my grandfather, Dr Patrick Playfair, who was Minister of the First Charge 1899–1924. In the second chapter there is an edited talk which my grandfather gave to the St Andrews Literary Society in 1902. It gives a brief history of the Town Kirk from the time it was built on the present site in South Street in 1412 to 1901 when a huge congregation was in church to mourn and commemorate the death of Queen Victoria. It was one of the last big occasions in the Nineteenth Century kirk. Some additional notes taken from *The Parish Church of the Holy Trinity, St Andrews* by Dr W. E. K. Rankin, Minister of the First Charge 1935–67 have been incorporated. The third chapter describes the Restoration project from inception to completion as the story unfolds in the Minutes of the General and Executive Committees.

The text is accompanied by a selection of photographs, some old and some new. For permission to reproduce images from the collections of St Andrews University Library Department of Special Collections and of Holy Trinity Church I am deeply indebted. Some images have been taken from my grandfather's collection of slides now in the St Andrews University Library Department of Special Collections Playfair archive. The contemporary photographs have been taken mainly by Peter Adamson and a few by Bridget, my wife. For these excellent illustrations I am most grateful.

Finally I would like to thank all those who have helped with advice and encouragement in the compilation of this commemorative book. Invaluable help and encouragement has come from Dr Norman Reid and Priscilla Jackson of the St Andrews University Library Department of Special Collections, and from the Revd Rory MacLeod, Minister and George Donaldson, Church Officer of Holy Trinity. Encouragement has come from John Rankin, son of Dr W. E. K. Rankin, former Minister of the First Charge of Holy Trinity, and from my wife and family. I am deeply indebted to Peter Adamson for his enthusiasm and professionalism. The quality of his photographs has enormously enhanced the text. I am also indebted to Mark Lawson of the Librario Press for without his advice and help the book would never have seen the light of day. For the inevitable shortcomings and errors I accept full responsibility, but it is my fond hope that this small offering will help to foster a renewal of interest in this superb church building and in the Gospel message which it proclaims. The late Ivor Bulmer-Thomas wrote: 'Churches are in themselves acts of worship; their message is delivered, not for half an hour on Sundays, but for every hour of every day of every year, and not merely to those who enter but to those who pass by. A beautiful and historic church fulfils its most useful purpose merely by existing – as a pointer to a world of spiritual values.'

Patrick Macdonald Playfair

Parish Minister, Master Builder

Dr Patrick Playfair was outstanding among the ministers of his generation. He made his name as Minister of the First Charge at Holy Trinity, St Andrews 1899–1924. Had it not been for ill health he would have been the eleventh Minister of Holy Trinity to become Moderator of the General Assembly of the Church of Scotland, for he was twice asked to take on this position of responsibility. A man of outward grandeur and inward simplicity, he may not have been a literary or intellectual giant, but he had a genius of his own based on common sense, practical ability, and devotion to duty. In his funeral service Professor Main of Glasgow University described him as a 'master builder'. 'It has been given to few Scots of modern times to earn so really and so worthily the Pauline epithet.' He referred to Playfair's outstanding qualities of loyalty, dignity, and friendliness. Dr Roger Kirkpatrick in his biography of Patrick Playfair concludes with an appropriate tribute: 'He was pre-eminently a great Parish Minister.' There were many tributes in the newspapers at the time of his death. Dr Archibald Fleming, in *The Times*, wrote of him as 'a scorner of prominence or fame. Duty was to him its own reward; and if his gifted tongue was ever mordant, it was at the expense of the self-seeker and the hunter after showy reputation. Yet, with all his humility, he indulged one deep absorbing pride. It was the Church of his fathers – her history, her martyrdoms, her struggle for freedom and right, her great share in making Scotland what she is.' Herbert Wiseman, his friend and organist at Holy Trinity 1908–21, wrote in the *Scotsman*: 'The passing of Dr Playfair of St Andrews, has removed one of the most striking figures which the Church of Scotland has produced in recent years.' Undoubtedly the qualities which brought him such fame were those of the compassionate friend and visitor and of the preacher of clarity and conviction. He had a tremendous capacity for work and getting things done. He attributed this ability to a meticulous concern for punctuality and the delivery of what he promised.

Patrick Macdonald Playfair was born in the manse of Abercorn, a country parish near Edinburgh on November 5th, 1858. His parents, the Revd David Playfair and Jane Pitcairn, had three other children who survived into adult life. David became a distinguished doctor in Bromley, Kent. Cecilia married the Revd William Vassie, Minister of Castleton in Liddesdale, and Alice died unmarried in Edinburgh. After schooling at Blair Lodge School, he went to Edinburgh University where he became Neil Arnott Scholar in Physics and Herbarium Gold Medallist. A keen botanist and scientist he might well have become a doctor like his elder brother, but instead he followed his father and became a minister in the Kirk. Four uncles by marriage were also ministers, two of them becoming Moderators – the Very Revd James Chrystal and the Very Revd K.M. Phin. Another, the Revd Charles Lyon, was Episcopalian priest in St Andrews and author of a *History of St Andrews*. The fourth, the Revd Dr Patrick Fairbairn, became Principal of the Free Church College, Glasgow after the Disruption in 1843.

In 1882 he became assistant to Dr Norman Macleod at St Stephen's, Edinburgh thus following in his father's footsteps for he too had been assistant at St Stephen's. It was, perhaps, the most renowned parish in Scotland and it served Patrick well. Norman Macleod held him in high esteem and treated him as a favoured son. It was largely through Norman Macleod that Patrick was appointed to Glencairn and later to Holy Trinity, St Andrews. He chose Patrick as his Moderator's chaplain and he spoke warmly of his role in the Restoration of Holy

Trinity at the lunch party following the Rededication Service on St Andrew's Day 1909. 'It demanded for its prosecution a rare combination of qualities – courage, boldness, tenacity of purpose, and tact.' It was while at St Stephen's that we see him at his robust and dutiful best. He was staying with his aunt and uncle at Castleton Manse when he was persuaded to take an evening service at Langholm church, some twelve miles away. With no prepared sermon, for he was on holiday, and with no transport available he walked the twelve miles and preached an extempore sermon, which won the admiration of the congregation present. On leaving St Stephen's the presentation of a silver salver testified to the affection and admiration with which he was regarded by both minister and congregation.

The appointment of Patrick as ordained Minister of Glencairn in 1886 began a happy and constructive ministry in this widespread rural parish. It included the village of Moniaive and it was the birthplace of the Covenanter James Renwick. The parish was entirely suited to Patrick's great love of the countryside and people, and it was a wonderful preparation for his future ministry in St Andrews. In thirteen years he made such a lasting impression that on the Sunday following his death in St Andrews in 1924 a memorial service was held in Glencairn Parish Church as well as in Holy Trinity, St Andrews. A mission church and hall were built in Moniaive and as Chairman of the Parish Council he was instrumental in helping to bring the railway to the village. At the opening of the Cairn Valley Railway in 1905 he was invited to give the toast of success to the venture. In 1891 he was chairman of a public meeting which voted overwhelmingly to oppose the politically motivated attempt to disestablish the Church and to press for the union of all Presbyterian Churches in Scotland. One speaker forcefully recalled Dr Thomas Chalmers' statement of 1843 that it was the Government's duty to support the ministry and teaching of the Gospel throughout the land.

It was at Glencairn that his three children were born, for in 1888 in St Stephen's, Edinburgh he had married Eliza, daughter of Edinburgh lawyer John Walker and his wife Margaret, daughter of Francis Maxwell of Gribton. Elma, the eldest, died unmarried, the last member of the Playfair family to live permanently in St Andrews. Patrick Lyon was killed in World War I, and Jack, who married Marjory Armour-Hannay, was father of the writer of these notes and an elder of Holy Trinity.

The death of the renowned Dr A.K.H. Boyd created the opportunity for Patrick to embark on the ministry which was to have such a profound effect on himself and upon Holy Trinity, St Andrews. For the second time in fifty years a minister from Glencairn was translated to Holy Trinity, St Andrews. The unanimous choice of the selection committee and overwhelmingly supported by the congregation, he was inducted as Minister of the First Charge in August 1899. The following Sunday he was introduced to the congregation by his friend and mentor Dr Norman Macleod, then Minister of Inverness. For Patrick it was a sort of homecoming for his great grandfather, Dr James Playfair had been Principal of the United College 1799–1819 and his great uncle Sir Hugh Lyon Playfair had been Provost of St Andrews 1842–61.

In St Andrews the main features of his ministry in Glencairn were repeated on a larger scale – regard for tradition and continuity, enthusiasm for progress and development, and a deep commitment to both the parish and the wider Church. Holy Trinity was a collegiate charge with two ministers responsible for the town church, St Mary's at the West end of Market Street, and a mission church in Boarhills. The first eighteen months were extremely busy and he established for himself a considerable reputation for visiting and preaching, the two attributes he deemed essential for successful ministry. In addition to parish duties he became Chaplain to the 6th Volunteer Battalion of the Black Watch, Moderator's Chaplain, and Chaplain to the Royal and Ancient Golf Club. By command he preached before Queen Victoria in October 1900. This, the first of three visits to Balmoral, proved a happy experience. At dinner in the evening the Queen congratulated him: 'You preached us an excellent sermon this morning and I hear you preached another excellent sermon in the parish church.' He had gone straight from Balmoral to morning service in Crathie church. He taught and befriended the young being especially involved with St Leonard's and St Katherine's Schools for Girls; he sang with the Holy Trinity choir and encouraged the organist and choirmaster, for he was an accomplished musician; and he actively supported missionary work both at home and abroad.

Within a short space of time Boarhills was established as a separate parish from Holy Trinity and the Church Halls in Greenside Place built at a cost of some £2,500. The latter were essential for carrying out the work of the Sunday School, Bible classes, the Girls' Guildry, the Women's Work Party, and other parish agencies. They were also necessary for the time when Holy Trinity was closed for restoration. It was in December 1901 that Patrick raised in Kirk Session the question of the condition of the fabric, which led to the decision to embark on complete restoration. There were of course other decisions to be made at that time and important events to be commemorated. The organist's salary was put up to £25 a year, the session clerk's salary was augmented by £5 due to the increased work load, the delivery of coal to poorer members was organised, and rubber shoes were bought for the beadle, Stewart Wilson so that he could walk quietly in the galleries during services. A lectern and font were gifted by the family in memory of Dr Boyd. Services in memory of Queen Victoria and in honour of the Coronation of Edward VII were organised. Stuart Grace, elder for over forty years, and Alexander Hunter, first sponsor of the Restoration with a gift of £1,000, died in 1902.

It must have been a huge relief to Patrick and his family when they moved in to Wyvern, their new home on the corner of City Road in 1906, for there was no proper manse at that time for the Minister of the First Charge. It was a substantial, well equipped house with staff quarters, photographic darkroom and so on. Over the front door there is incised the inscription, *Pax intrantibus, salus exeuntibus* (Peace to those who enter, health and prosperity to those who leave). Detailed accounts show that the work cost some £4,000. The manse for the Minister of the Second Charge was 156 South Street. Relations between the two ministers were entirely happy in Patrick's day. However, there were five vacancies in the Ministry of the Second Charge, each one lasting at least six months. Especially difficult were the latter years of World War I when the Revd Kenneth Grant was away on duty with the army in France and in Macedonia. Sunday services had still to be taken morning and evening in both Holy Trinity and St Mary's (services in the latter church were eventually suspended), besides all the other parish cares and duties.

The Kirk Session Minutes give some indication of the extent of work involved throughout Patrick's ministry. There were appointments to be made – new elders, the organist and choirmaster, the parish sister, beadles, and caretakers for the Church Halls. Property had to be looked after – the 156 South Street (a replacement manse 17 Queen's Gardens was bought for £1,580 in 1924), New Park, Law Park (sold to Philip Boase for £3,500 in 1923), St Mary's Church (closed for worship in 1918), the Church Halls (lets and repairs to vandalised windows), as well as the restored Holy Trinity Church. Bequests, trusts, and government business (Childrens and National Insurance Acts) required attention – a resolution demanding the inclusion of Religious Instruction as an integral part of education in all schools was sent to the Prime Minister, the Secretary of State, and the local MP in 1918. These are just some of the matters which had to be dealt with apart from the pastoral and liturgical duties of the ministers.

The Restoration was, of course, a huge enterprise which absorbed an enormous amount of his time and energy. Although a sub-committee was formed to supervise the final weeks of the work no committee meeting was held between May 1907 and April 1909. During this period nearly all matters connected with the Restoration fell on the shoulders of Patrick and the treasurer of the project, his cousin Charles Stuart Grace. His patience, energy and meticulous attention to detail were exemplary. The organ builder once said: "He's a terror, that parson. If he comes here much oftener, he'll know as much about organ building as I do." But there was a price to be paid. In 1906 he embarked on an extensive cruise to the West Indies on the advice of his doctors. Again on doctors' advice he visited Madeira with his daughter Elma in 1910, joined another cruise in 1911, and visited North America in 1913. On all these holidays, including others in France, the Channel Islands, and the Netherlands, he took a keen interest in all that he saw and in all the people he met. On returning to St Andrews he lectured to fascinated audiences using his own lantern slides and copious notes. While in New York he preached on three consecutive Sundays in Rutger's Presbyterian Church on the intersection of Broadway and 73rd Street.

The restored Holy Trinity Church was dedicated on St Andrew's Day 1909. Although the Presbytery had wanted him to preach on that important occasion the honour fell to the Moderator, the Rt Revd James Robertson, Minister of Whittingehame, whose connection with St Andrews gave him additional reason for fulfilling this role – he had played golf with Allan Robertson and he was a friend of Tom Morris. The Restoration was quite as successful as everyone involved had hoped. It was indeed a treasure house of interest. 'Growth there must always be – growth at least as regards adaptation, equipment, ornament, beauty.' Patrick's were no idle words. When embryo plans were being made in 1901 there were 1,037 communicants at the November Communion service in Holy Trinity. At the Communion service following the Rededication there were 1,262 communicants. The numbers of both worshippers and visitors increased. In 1913 there were 1,677 communicants and between July and September 1912 there were 15,000 weekday visitors. Giving was more generous. The organ was enhanced and stained glass windows, particularly Douglas Strachan's East and West windows, were installed to add to the three stained glass windows which existed at the time of the Rededication. There were other duties and commitments for Patrick. In 1912 he became President of the Glasgow Society of the Sons of Ministers of the Church of Scotland, and on St Andrew's Day that year there was a special service to commemorate the 500th anniversary of Holy Trinity church on the present site.

Inevitably, the outbreak of war in 1914 added significantly to Patrick's burden. It was not simply the absence of a colleague for several months, but the whole business of anxiety, sorrow and hardship. "Do not let us forget prayer," he said. Throughout the war years there was a daily service in Holy Trinity. 'Do not let us grow weary of seeking God's help for our Nation … what is mere inconvenience when we think of these awful trenches?' His sermons during the war years were full of a sense of patriotic duty and the need for economy, sentiments which seem foreign to contemporary ears. Early in 1915 his friend and assistant at Holy Trinity for eight months in 1907, the young parish minister of Elie, William Monteith, son of his predecessor at Glencairn, who had enlisted as a trooper in the local Yeomanry, was killed in action. It was a grievous blow for only a short time before he had officiated at William's marriage to Muriel Cox in Largo Church. "No one," he said, "in our land has any right to expect to come out of this time of war without loss of any kind." His elder son Lyon was reported wounded and missing at Lestrem in France in April 1918 though it was not until March 1919 that all hope was abandoned that he might be still alive. Characteristically he sold the much prized family heirloom, a fifteenth century Book of Hours (now in the Victoria and Albert Museum as a condition of purchase) to Mr Otto Beit for £100 in order to help Red Cross funds. There were other ways in which he practised what he preached. He gave up his smoking and he worked for an hour before breakfast every day in the garden at Wyvern adding the cultivation of vegetables to that of his beloved flowers.

With the war over parish life gradually returned to normal. The salaries of the beadle and Herbert Wiseman the organist, recently returned from war service, were put up by £20 per annum. There were memorials to be erected and national reconstruction and rededication to be considered. Replicas of the City War Memorial panels were put up in the South transept, and the clerestory windows were appropriately dedicated. A service was held in April 1919 to support the mission for National Rededication. In the parish magazine, which he instituted at the beginning of his ministry he wrote: 'We did not cry in vain to God for deliverance from our enemies in the war hardly yet closed; He will be with us still if we seek His help and devote ourselves to His service in all sincerity of heart. All is not well.' There were important visitors to welcome – Marcel Dupré, organist of Notre Dame, Paris who gave a recital in 1921, Earl Haig in 1921 and 1922, the Prince of Wales in 1922. After twenty-one years of service on the Council of St Leonard's School he became Chairman in 1922. Towards the end of the war Patrick accepted the post of Convenor of the General Assembly's Committee on Correspondence with the Scottish Synod in England. This involved visits to Scottish congregations in England as well as meetings in London. By now, however, there was serious concern for his health. Mention has already been made of his pre-war holidays taken on medical advice. Apart from post-war holidays in the Highlands and England he went to Duff House, Banff and Ruthin in Wales for treatment. His last holidays were spent with his son Jack in Madeira in 1923 and in the Channel Islands in 1924. Always he regarded these occasions as opportunities for furthering his interests in botany in particular but also in places and people in general.

In the autumn of 1924 Patrick was admitted to the St Andrews Cottage Hospital for what was assumed to be a fairly routine operation on an injury to his foot. At first all appeared to be going well but the operation affected his weakened condition. He died peacefully at his home, Wyvern on October 6. So ended the life of this greatly admired and loved man.

Tributes had been paid and honours had been bestowed upon him during his lifetime, especially in 1909–10 following the completion of the Restoration. He had been made an honorary Doctor of Divinity by St Andrews University in 1909. He had three times preached at Crathie – before Queen Victoria at Balmoral once and before George V and Queen Mary in Crathie Church in 1912 and 1919. Twice he had been invited to become Moderator of the Kirk. These tributes were as nothing compared to the tributes which came following his death. Instead of celebrating twenty-five years of his ministry and inducting the Revd A.S. Dunlop as Minister of the Second Charge the parish mourned the passing of their minister. The funeral service was conducted by the Revd Kenneth Grant, Patrick's last and valued colleague, by Mr Wallace of St Leonard's, who had given invaluable assistance over the latter years, and by Dr Cathels, Moderator of the General Assembly. The preacher, Professor Main of Glasgow University and formerly of St Mary's College, gave the congregation an example of his sense of duty. 'King's College, Cambridge, the College of Dr Playfair's gallant son, Lyon, observed its Service of Commemoration of the fallen on a day of Holy Communion in your Church. A short time before that Sunday, and in one of the few moments of self-revelation which our friend permitted himself, I learned how much he longed to be present at that sadly memorable service. At once I pled that his brothers of St Mary's College should come to his aid, but every argument was in vain. "My duty on that day is to be with my own congregation".' The Church was packed with family, friends, and representatives of all the bodies, local and national, with which he had been associated. The funeral procession stretched from the door of Holy Trinity along the length of South Street to the West door of the ruined Cathedral. He was buried in the family vault in the Eastern Cemetery. The General Assembly report of 1925 included a memorable tribute, part of which follows: 'Absorbed in the work of his parish and in its great claims upon him, he found little leisure to take part in the general affairs of the Church. But no Minister of his time was held in higher honour for his fine personal qualities and for his work's sake than was Patrick Macdonald Playfair.'

In his memory funds were raised to establish a peal of bells to replace the existing bells which were of no special value. On St Andrew's Day 1926 a peal of fifteen bells cast by John Taylor and Company of Loughborough was dedicated by his biographer, Dr Roger Kirkpatrick, Minister of Yarrow. There is also a window to the memory of Patrick and his wife Eliza by Douglas Strachan in the North aisle given by their surviving children, Jack and Elma. His portrait by Douglas Strachan hangs in St Mary's College.

Bibliography

The Ministry of Patrick Macdonald Playfair by Roger S. Kirkpatrick
Kirk Session Minutes.
Notes, diaries, and cuttings in the family archive

Paper on the Town Church

Given to the Literary Society by the Revd Patrick Playfair on February 12, 1902

Many of us are now interested in the Parish or Town Church or Church of the Holy Trinity, so I thought I would depart from the usual style of address and offer some disjointed remarks upon that building – remarks which will be neither exhaustive nor erudite but such as anyone might throw together with the aid of a few books and in a few hours.

The name 'Town' Church is not very old, but it has been in use for at least 140 years. It is a curious term and I know of only two other places where the same name is used. In both St Peter Port, Guernsey and St Helier, Jersey the Parish Church is known as the Town Church.

Three derivations of the term are obvious. It may have been called the Town Church as opposed to the Cathedral – the church of the citizens as opposed to that of the religious orders; or the Town Church as opposed to the College Church; or through its position in the middle of the town (the cathedral being outside the town in its own precincts).

At one time the Parish Church too was outside the town beside the cast gable of the Cathedral. *The Church of Holy Trinity was dedicated in 1243 and joined three other churches in the area – the Culdee Church, St Rule's, and the Cathedral.* But in 1412 a new Parish Church was founded where it now stands. *Sir William Lindsay gave the land on which the new church was built – six rigs (180 feet wide) from South Street towards Market Street, but not the full length of the rigs, between Logie's Wynd and Kirk Wynd. The seventh rig to the west, where Church Square stands, was given to the Church by Bishop Wardlaw in 1430.*

Why should there be a Parish Church at all with a huge Cathedral already completed and dedicated 100 years before 1412? A Cathedral has purposes of its own. It was the central ecclesiastical building of the diocese and many ceremonies, celebrations and processions took place in it which had only indirect concern with the parish. It must have also been used by members of the neighbouring religious orders. The Revd C.J. Lyon estimates that at the Reformation there were at least 160 ecclesiastics and monks in St Andrews. The practice of hiring priests to say masses for the dead was greatly on the increase and it may have been thought necessary to provide more altars for the townsfolk. There was a Town Altar in the Cathedral but there was demand for more. Furthermore the Parish Church may have been designed for preaching before that aid to religion went out of fashion.

For whatever reason the new Parish Church was built on the new site. *Dr W.E.K. Rankin suggests a number of reasons for the building of the new Town Kirk – growth in population, dilapidation of the existing building which was in any case unsuited to the fifteenth century fashion for a multiplicity of altars (thirty-two or thirty-three in the new church) to help the faithful achieve safe passage through the pains of Purgatory, and to assist in the battle against heresy and pestilence, and to get away from the Cathedral.* It was evidently a plain but dignified building – impressive but in no way vying with the Cathedral. Its outline is shown in two old maps dated 1530 and 1642, and recent examination of the present building proves their accuracy. It was a three-aisled building with side aisles separated by two arcades of nine arches, on which rested the clerestory wall which in turn supported the central roof. Two transepts extended north and south from the fourth and fifth bays counting from the east. One of them still standing we know as the Communion Aisle, but it may not have been part of the original design. We understand that there were no less than thirty altars, each one endowed and with at least one attached chaplain, whose business it was to say masses for the souls of the dead. There were also fifteen choristers, who seemed to have formed a guild with a seal of their own bearing the device of a skull and crossbones referring to the dead for whose benefit they chanted.

That is very unlike the Town Church as it is now. It seems to have fallen into disrepair. The altars of course were swept away at the Reformation. Little was done to keep it in order and the whole outside appearance was changed as we see from Oliphant's sketch of 1767. It might still have been like that but for the desire of the landward Heritors to increase the seating capacity from their current 120 sittings. After twelve years of legal wrangling with the Town Council, the University and the Incorporated Trades the rebuilding of the church began under the supervision of Edinburgh architect James Salisbury *(in fact the architect was Robert Balfour)* on March 3rd, 1798. The aim was to increase the seating capacity as cheaply as possible at whatever cost to the old masonry. The Lord Ordinary said: "The proposed accommodation of removing pillars in an ancient Gothic edifice is inadmissible, and to which the Ordinary will in no sort append his sanction." The Lord President, Islay Campbell, wrote in the margin of his copy of the case: 'No pillars ought to be removed. The proof shows that this might be attended with risk as the pillars support the roof.' At least four pillars were removed, the height and pitch of the roof altered, the side aisle roofs abolished, the walls taken down to the ground, or nearly so, except only the west gable, and the present high walls and gables built instead. The result was the addition of some 800 sittings and the complete alteration of the Church. All that remains of the 1412 Church is the tower, west gable, two west bays of each arcade, and the foundations.

In 1412 Wardlaw had just founded the University. The kingdom was under the Regent, Robert Stewart, Duke of Albany – young James I being a prisoner in England. So the Town Church started side by side with the University, when the throne was empty and the Roman Church in full power.

It was founded amidst the first rumblings of the Reformation – the storm which did much damage but cleared the unhealthy atmosphere. John Resby had been burned at Perth five years before. Paul Craw was burned in St Andrews twenty-one years later. The masons would still be building the Church when on February 3rd, 1414 they would pause in their work to watch the great procession with over 400 clergy moving through the nave of the Cathedral to the altar in celebration of Henry Ogilvy's return from Rome with Pope Benedict XIII's Bull confirming the establishment of the University. It was a great day in the Cathedral and a day of rejoicing in the town with the ringing of bells and at night bonfires and universal festivity.

Many strange scenes have been enacted around and within the Town Church since it was built and at some of these we may glance.

Before the Reformation the Town Church was overshadowed by the Cathedral but in June 1559 it was rendered useless for worship. The Parish Church then became the centre of Church life. In 1530 it had become a preaching place for those advocating a purer religion 'against pride and the idle life of Bishops and against the abuses of the whole ecclesiastical estate'. Friar William Arth preached a sermon on the theme 'Verity is the strongest of all things'. Patrick Hamilton had been burned in front of St Salvator's College in 1528.

In 1547 John Knox came from East Lothian and took up residence in the Castle. He brought with him three pupils. 'Besydis thare grammare, and other humane authoris, he redd unto thame a catechisme, a compt whairof he caused thame publictlie in the parishe Kirk of Sanctandrois.' He also preached so impressively on St John's Gospel in the Castle chapel that he was asked to be their preacher in place of John Rough who, though sincere and earnest, was not enough of a theologian to tackle the scholars of the University. Dean John

Annan had long troubled Rough but now he found more than his match in Knox and being beaten on all fronts took refuge in the Church's authority, 'which damned all Lutherans and heretics; and therefore he needeth no further disputation'. Knox's reply was a public challenge from the pulpit of the Parish Church 'to prove the Roman Church this day farther degenerate from the purity which was in the days of the Apostles, than was the Church of the Jews from the ordinance given by Moses, when they consented to the innocent death of Jesus Christ'. The people hearing the challenge cried with one voice: 'We cannot all read from writtingis butt we may all hear your preaching: Tharefore we requyre yow, in the name of God, that ye will lett us hear the probatioun of that which ye have affirmed; for yf it be trew we have been miserable deceaved.' The next Sunday Knox preached and we can be sure that the Kirk was full with a congregation including his former teacher John Major, 'the most famous teacher of his day in Scotland' according to John Hume, members of the University, many Canons, and some Friars. No doubt everyone kept awake that day!

The sermon was favourably received by his friends but the highest compliment was paid by his enemies who arranged that every learned man in the Abbey and University was to preach in the Parish Church upon the Lord's day. So Knox had to be content with the weekdays.

In 1551 the Prior of the Black Friars urged people to pray using the Lord's Prayer (Pater Noster) only to God and not to Saints or any other creature. The University and the Grey Friars objected and one of their number preached on November 1st, 1551 that people should pray to Saints, but with little effect. He merely provoked a violent schism within the Kirk and earned himself the nickname 'Friar Pater Noster', 'who, at the last, being convicted in his owne conscience and ashamed of his former sermoun, was compelled to leave the toun of Sanct Andrewes'.

Another incident involving Knox concerned the execution of a witch. James Melville, Minister of Anstruther, wrote in his diary about a witch he once saw set against a pillar in the Kirk while Knox dealt with her from the pulpit. Of all uncomfortable situations I think that of being set against a pillar in the Town Kirk of St Andrews in the midst of a fiery and bloodthirsty congregation with that unsparing tongue of Knox flaying you and hurling at you all manner of horrible prophecies must have been the worst. To be thrown into the Witch's Lake to drown would be welcome relief!

Knox's last visit is described by James Melville. 'Being in St Androis he was verie weak. I saw him everie day of his doctrine go hulie and fear (slowly and warily), with a furring of martricks about his neck, a staff in the an hand, and guid godlie Richart Ballanden, his servand, halding upe the uther oxtar (shoulder) from the Abbay to the Paroche Kirk, and be the said Richart and another servant lifted upe to the pulpit, whar he behovit to lean at his first entrie; bot or he haid done with his sermont he was sa active and vigorus that he was lyk to ding that pulpit in blads, and fly out of it'. Shortly after, in 1572, he died in Edinburgh.

The same year John Douglas was appointed the first post-Reformation Archbishop of St Andrews. His appointment was irregular, some say invalid, but he held office for four years. Patrick Adamson would fain have had it and showed his spleen in a sermon in the Town Church when he classified bishops as 'My Lord Bischop, My Lord's Bischop, and The Lord's Bischop', (the Papal bishop, the nobleman's bishop, and the true faithful minister of the Gospel). He soon became a Bishop, a nobleman's Bishop, a talchan. One account says Douglas was of great eloquence and piety; another says he was remiss and neglected his preaching. But he appears to have been in bad health and the end came tragically in the pulpit of the Parish Church. Goaded by taunts hurled at him as an 'unpreaching prelate' he made a last effort, exerted himself beyond his strength, sank down and died. He was buried in the ground round the Church under a mound, without any inscription or monument.

Douglas was succeeded by Patrick Adamson, evidently an unpopular man although called by George Martine 'a most famous and faithful preacher of the Holy Word'. He kept himself in the Castle 'lyk a tod in his holl', sick of some dreadful disease and often under the care of a woman suspected of witchcraft. 'But verelie,' writes James Melville, 'about these witches we war plane and scharpe with him, bathe from pulpit, in doctrine, and be censur of our Presbyterie.' There was no favour shown even to Bishops if suspected of witchcraft. Only when King James VI came, not long after, did he occupy the pulpit and, anxious to please His Majesty, he affirmed that the report that the Duke of Lennox had died a Romanist was false, and flourished a scroll which he called 'the Duke, his testament' to show he died a good Protestant. But an honest merchant woman saw it and affirmed it was 'a compt of a four or fyve yeir aul dett that a few days befor sche haid send to him; wharof she gat no mair payment nor the Duc his executors maid hir'. There was no love lost between Andrew Melville (uncle of James) and Patrick Adamson. Melville called him 'empoisoned with the venom of an old serpent; a cockatrice egg full of falsehood, malice and knavery'. 'Mr Andrew' was not a man to injure, for he was a hard hitter and had many friends. Yet the Bishop excommunicated James and Andrew Melville and others. True they had first excommunicated him so it was tit for tat. He penned an excommunication and 'in a bischoplie maner send out a boy with ane or twa of his jakmen (servants), and red the sam in the Kirk … which was as much thought on, even among the people, as if he had spat in the Kirk'. Next Sunday he came to the Church and was about to mount the pulpit when someone came and told him that a number of gentlemen were convened outside intending to take him from the pulpit and hang him. 'Wharat, calling for his jakmen and frinds to byde about him, he reased a grait tumult in the Kirk, and for feir could nocht byd in the kirk, but tuk him to the stiple; out of the quhilk, be the balyies, accompanied with all his favorars and friends, skarslie could he be drawin to be convoyed saifflie to his awin Castell'. However he was 'half ruggit' out and borne away. James Melville reported an astonishing event: 'For veritie to me be manie honest men that saw it with their eis that a heare brak amangs the multitude in the middes of the common Hiegett and streit, and ran befor tham toward the Castell, and down throw the Northgett. This the vulgar callit the Bischope's witch! But after all the pother there was not the slightest appearance of tumult in the city.' Adamson died in extreme poverty in 1592 neglected by the King and former friends, some say helped by Melville.

Andrew Melville too had incident in the Town Church. The Session used to ask the two Melvilles, who held University posts, to help them on the Sabbath in the absence of both a minister and the Bishop. 'Mr Andro with ane herociall spreit, the mair they stirit and bostit the mair he strak with the two-eagit sword: sa that a day he movit the Provost, with sear rubbin of the ga' of his conscience, to ryse out of his seat in the middes of the sermont, and with sum muttering of words to goe to the dure, out throw the middes of the people. For the quhilk, being dealt with by the Presbytery and convicted in his conscience' the said Provost made public satisfaction 'by acknowledging of his offence, and craving God and the congregation forgiffness.' They were pulpit giants in those days!

When the Presbytery eventually released James and Andrew from pulpit supply, two town rulers wrote a disgruntled paper which was read in the Church by the 'taker up of the Psalms' i.e. precentor, who was called before the Presbytery and 'got his reward for he never throve nor did good after that but died with madness and misery'.

The two town rulers went before the General Assembly and were ordered to do public penance before Mr Andrew in the Kirk, which they did and became 'better conditioned thereafter'. Perhaps they stood on the stools of repentance. Some years afterwards as Robert Wallace, one of the ministers of St Andrews, was preaching in the Parish Church to the King he was interrupted by His Majesty, whereupon Andrew rebuked the King and threatened him with the judgement of God if he did not repent. We cannot hope that the stool of repentance was ever graced by royal foot! James Melville states that at the very time that the King interrupted Andrew Wallace there was an earthquake which made all the north parts of Scotland tremble. This reminded many of King Uzziah offering incense on the Golden Altar. But the earthquake did not shake the Parish Church of St Andrews, where the offender was. It is interesting to note that there has always been a royal pew in the Parish Church – presently occupied by the Town magistrates. *(It was surrendered by the Crown in 1909)*.

We must hurry on. In *Twenty-five Years of St Andrews* Dr Boyd refers to three Archbishops buried in the Town Church – James Sharp, George Gladstanes, and a third I cannot identify. Douglas, as I have said, was buried outside. Burial in kirks had been prohibited by the Assembly of 1588, but like many other Acts of Assembly it does not seem to have been observed. Gladstanes was made Archbishop in December 1610, but in the previous October he held, as Bishop of Fife, a Diocesan Synod in the aisle of the Kirk. It seems he was fond of ease and customarily preached only in the forenoon while in the afternoon he enjoyed some pastime or lay on his bed and slept. He died on May 2nd, 1615 in the Castle. The description given of his death by David Calderwood is disgusting. He died of some terrible disease which made necessary immediate burial in the Parish Church. Archbishop Spottiswoode, his successor, says he was buried in the south-east aisle of the parish Church; Martine says he was buried in the 'Communion Aisle'. The formal funeral took place on June 7th but it was a windy, stormy day and the canopy of black velvet borne above the empty coffin by four men was carried away by the wind thus marring the ceremony. Two years later we have a glimpse of King James VI in the porch of the Parish Church (another part which has disappeared) listening to a speech in Latin by the Principal of St Leonard's College.

In 1639, the year that Archbishop Spottiswoode died, Samuel Rutherford came to St Andrews and often he must have preached in the Parish Church. An English merchant who heard him there writes: 'a little fair man who showed me the loveliness of Christ'.

On April 16th, 1662 James Sharp, formerly Minister of Crail, came to St Andrews as Archbishop appointed by King Charles II. He was attended by many horsemen and rode between two nobles all the way from Leslie. The Sabbath after he arrived he preached in the Town Church. His text was a remarkable one, 'For I determined to know nothing among you, save Jesus Christ and Him crucified', in which he vindicated himself and the Episcopalian Church. On May 16th, 1679 James Sharp or rather his corpse was again escorted to the Town Church thirteen days after he had been murdered. It was a tremendous procession of leaders and representatives of Church and State headed by sixty-one old men, corresponding to the deceased's age. The coach from which he was dragged was also there, and the bloody gown he had worn. His mitre rested on a velvet cushion on the coffin and over it a canopy borne by six Moderators of Presbyteries. The Church was decked in full mourning and the Bishop of Edinburgh preached the sermon. The body was laid in the grave to the sound of trumpets. It was a great scene.

We pass on 222 years. The Church has been completely altered, but somewhere beneath its floor lies all that is left of George Gladstanes and against its aisle wall stands the monument to the memory of

James Sharp. A great crowd throngs the building. Far away, all the wealth and chivalry of Britain are gathered to lay in the ground the mortal remains of Victoria the Good; but here, without pomp and pageantry, there is an outpouring of thanks for her great life and pious example. Silently and sorrowfully thousands have come to pay homage to God for His gift and to express their devotion to her who has gone; silently they go away but the scene will never fade from their memories.

It seems to me that the Church which has witnessed all these and many more scenes is worth preserving, worth restoring to its ancient simple dignity – if only for the wonderful amount of local and national history it has helped to make. But far more than that, because it is the House of God and should be exceedingly magnificent.

P.S. Founders of the Literary Society in 1838 included the brothers William Davidson and Hugh Lyon Playfair, great uncles of Patrick Playfair. The Society collapsed in 1909.

The words in italics have been added by the editor.

Further reading:

The Parish Church of Holy Trinity, St Andrews, PreReformation by
    W.E.K. Ranking D.D.
The Parish Church of the Holy Trinity, St Andrews by Ronald G. Cant.

The Story of the Restoration
of Holy Trinity

'One must be thankful that the work was done when and how it was. It gave back to St Andrews the authentic form of its ancient *Town Kirk* at the very heart of the medieval city in a way that would scarcely have been possible at any earlier or later date'. There can be no doubt of the truth of the words of Ronald Cant, Reader in Medieval History at St Andrews University, written in 1970. For it was only at the beginning of the twentieth century that the need was accepted and the resources and leadership were available for such a momentous undertaking. After World War I it would have been well nigh impossible.

Restoration was first mooted in 1868 when the Very Revd Dr A.K.H. Boyd was Minister of the First Charge. Until 1978 there were two collegiate ministers of Holy Trinity. Dr Boyd's dream, unrealistic in his day, came to be fulfilled when the Revd Dr Patrick Macdonald Playfair became Minister of the First Charge in 1899 following the death of Dr Boyd the same year. In December 1901 Dr Playfair raised in Kirk Session the question of the condition of the fabric. It was then decided to restore the church to its historic medieval character as far as evidence and contemporary need allowed. For in 1798–1800 the medieval church built in 1410–12 had been completely remodelled as a galleried preaching arena by the architect Robert Balfour in order that the Heritors could seat the recommended number of parishioners, some 2,200 folk, two-thirds of the *examinable persons* (adult population) of St Andrews. Many described the new building in most unflattering terms – as 'destructive', an act of vandalism in which only the tower and the two western bays of the nave remained. The Kirk Session asked Dr Playfair to convene a committee to organise a public meeting to discuss the restoration of the church.

The public meeting duly took place in the Town Hall on January 10th, 1902. With the town's Provost in the Chair the meeting was addressed by the Very Revd Dr Marshall, Principal of Aberdeen University and a unanimous resolution passed to proceed with a scheme of restoration 'from the points of view of beauty, comfort and suitability'. A General Committee and a powerful Executive Committee were formed. The latter included Lord Balfour of Burleigh as Honorary President, Sir Ralph Anstruther Bt. as President, seven Vice-Presidents and a dozen or so committee members, numbers fluctuating as some died and others were co-opted. The leading members were Dr Playfair and his cousin Charles Stuart Grace, who acted as Honorary Treasurer.

Nearly eight years later, on St Andrew's Day 1909, the restored church was rededicated at a service in which the Moderator of the General Assembly, the Right Revd Dr James Robertson, Minister of Whittingehame preached. In those intervening years a huge amount of work had to be undertaken – plans made, scrutinized and approved; money raised; contractors and craftsmen appointed and supervised; alternative arrangements made for services in the newly built Parish Church Halls and St Mary's Church on the western extension of Market Street. This involved seven meetings of the General Committee and twenty meetings of the Executive Committee with a similar number of meetings of a Sub-Committee set up to decide and supervise details of the several aspects of the project – floors, roofs, windows, screens, stalls, pews, carvings and so on – once building work, which began in the Summer of 1907, was well under way. The Sub-Committee, consisting of Dr Playfair, Principal Alexander Stewart, Professor John Herkless (Professor of Church History and later Provost of St Andrews and Principal of the University), the Revd William Leathem, Minister of the Second Charge, and Messrs C.S. Grace and James Gillespie (Kirk Session representative at Heritors'

Meetings), was appointed and started its work of supervision in April 1909, only seven months before the rededication.

At the first meeting of the Executive Committee in the Session House of the old church on January 20th, 1902 it was 'unanimously resolved to invite plans for the restoration of the Town Church from Mr MacGregor Chalmers of Glasgow'. Already a generous gift of £1,000 had been promised by Alexander Hunter, who died in July 1902 and after whom the Hunter Memorial Aisle was named, towards the carrying out of a 'satisfactory scheme'. On April 19th, 1902 the General Committee unanimously approved 'generally of the plans for the restoration of the Town Church submitted by Mr MacGregor Chalmers and resolved to take all the necessary steps for carrying out the scheme'. By July the Heritors, whose duty it was to see that the church building was adequate for the size of the population, had agreed the scheme with appropriate conditions. Principal Stewart and Professor Lawson agreed to draw up a suitable prospectus appealing for funds. In the event nearly all the funds raised were by private subscription. A meeting was arranged with the Town Council, who in former days appointed and helped towards the stipend of the Minister of the Second Charge, to agree the extent of additions to the north of the church in order to avoid impeding access to the Fire Station, then located in Church Square.

The choice of Peter MacGregor Chalmers as architect was most felicitous, though inevitably in such a big scheme there was some dispute at the end of the contract over fees and other costs. The Baird Trustees found the architect's fee of £1,480 and some other items of expenditure 'most excessive' and the Executive Committee, perhaps not unreasonably, objected to the charge of £3.3s. for attendance at the Rededication Service. The architect insisted that he was entitled to up to £2,200, which included a sum for the Clerk of Works, as allowed in the original estimate of April 1907 for a total of

£21,253.2s.3d. The final cost was £23,793.7s.4d. In the end the architect agreed to waive a fee of £3.3s and any interest accruing 'in the interests of the Church as a whole and to avoid a dispute which could only have unfortunate results for all concerned'. The total cost of the restoration, including windows, organ, and other furnishings was some £30,000.

MacGregor Chalmers was well known for his church work, which included the restoration of Abercorn Church in West Lothian in 1893, where Dr Playfair's father had been Minister. Locally he had already designed the new St Leonard's Church in St Andrews dedicated in 1904 and he was responsible for the restoration of St Monans Church. Ronald Cant admired the architectural competence of MacGregor Chalmers, in particular his scholarship and taste. A completely faithful restoration of the medieval church was not possible because most of the building had been demolished in the 1798–1800 rebuild. Much evidence of the general appearance and of the detail of the medieval building was therefore lost, though the west end remained and a view of the church by John Oliphant in 1767 was of some help. The 1798–1800 walls had to be taken down and rebuilt for they were too slender to include appropriately moulded doorways and windows. Significant extensions were also required mainly to satisfy the Heritors' requirement to seat as many folk as possible in order to make up for the loss of seating capacity caused by the pulling down of the galleries. There was much debate about the seating capacity and eventually seating for 1,884 was agreed. On either side of the north transept a vestry and organ chamber were built, and on either side of the south transept, wherein lay the monumental tomb of Archbishop Sharp, a session house, where there may have been a medieval chapel, and a memorial chapel were added to the existing footprint. Dr Playfair had particularly wanted a chapel with chairs rather than pews in the south-east corner of the church.

In the restored church such medieval stone as could be salvaged from the 1798–1800 building was used in the core of the walls, but the dressed facing stone came for the Cullaloe quarry in West Fife as there was no longer any sandstone of suitable quality available from the Nydie and other local quarries. For the roofs Caithness flagstone was used. The architect borrowed many ideas from other buildings mainly in Scotland though the great east window was modelled on the east window of Carlisle cathedral only with seven rather than nine lights. The west doorway was derived from the burgh churches of Dundee and Haddington; the west window of five lancets from the seven-lancet window of St Machar's Cathedral, Aberdeen; the south porch from St Michael's, Linlithgow; the coved timber ceiling from King's College Chapel, Aberdeen; the clerestorey windows from Stirling Castle; and other decorative details from Iona Abbey, Dryburgh Abbey, Holy Rood, Stirling, and St Leonard's Chapel, St Andrews. All these features remarkable for their craftsmanship helped to re-establish Holy Trinity as one of the great burgh churches of Scotland. Ronald Cant wrote of the decorative work both within and without the church: 'The ornamental detail is of quite remarkable freshness and beauty.' In his sermon to mark the Jubilee of the Restoration in 1959 the Revd Dr John Wilson Baird, Minister of the Second Charge (1926–34) and later of St Machar's, Aberdeen said: "It is just fifty years now since … this ancient Church of the Holy Trinity arose from its degradation, and glowed and shone with a lustrous beauty and a Christian meaning probably greater than it had ever known."

Before building work began in the summer of 1907 the Executive Committee was mainly concerned with the raising and investing of funds. By November 1906 £19,480 had been promised. The Playfair family funded the north transept; the Baird Trust promised £2,000 on condition that the building was completed by the end of 1909 – in fact it was to contribute a further £500; a John Knox anniversary was used and a promise made to identify part of the building with his name – this turned out to be the south porch; the Women's Work Party contributed £2,000; St Leonard's and St Katharine's schools and the Sunday School funded the pillars in the south-east chapel; several stained glass windows were promised; and a letter of appeal sent out by the veteran golfer and Elder Tom Morris proved successful. Funds were invested carefully in dated Corporation, Utility and Railway Stocks. But plans for the new building were also considered, for the architect had been asked to submit working drawings 'at his convenience'. These had to be studied, discussed and amended.

In May 1907 estimates from the various contractors were received and approved. Many local firms were used – Andrew Thom and Sons, joiners; Thomas Black, slater; J.M. Morris, plumber; Dewar and Robertson, painters. But specialist firms of national standing were also employed – from Glasgow J.H. White and Sons, stone masons; S. Adams junior, glazier; A. McKay and Sons, wood carvers; and from England Willis and Son, organ builders. There were also heating engineers, electricians and marble workers. All worked under the direction of William Scott, clerk of works. The most notable individual craftsmen and artists were the stone carver James Young and the stained glass artists Douglas Strachan, Louis Davis, and James Powell and Sons. One of the joiners working for Andrew Thom was Alec Webster, who succeeded his father as beadle 1936–60. He made the font in the Hunter aisle out of remnants of oak from the Restoration roof. John Webster, his father, was appointed beadle in 1909 with an annual salary of £80. He had previously been beadle of St Mary's Church and keeper of the Church Halls.

The last service in the old church was held on June 2nd, 1907. Thereafter the builders moved in and services and meetings moved to the Parish Church Halls. From April 1909 the appointed Sub-Committee became fully involved with many matters of detail – the position of the organ console with advice from the organist Herbert Wiseman; the construction of the onyx, alabaster and Iona marble pulpit in memory of Dr Boyd; the detailing of the chancel screens and the ceiling, which was to be of oak rather than of pine as originally intended; the corbels in the session house representing St Andrews notables; the floors, windows and pews – the allocation of the pews to be made by Dr Playfair and Mr Grace for the pews in the old church, as was the custom, had been individually rented out to individuals and organisations, such as the Town Council, and litigation was to be avoided at all costs; the line of the railings and the material for the pavement outside with the Town Council, both parties agreeing to share the extra cost of stone rather than concrete. Three hundred chairs for the Hunter chapel from A. McKay and Sons at 7s.9d each were approved. Insurance was arranged. The session house safes which had been put in upside down were to be put right at no extra cost. A face on one of the capitals in the Hunter chapel was to be made more attractive. James Young's carvings were agreed for £650. Decorative designs produced by the architect were rejected. In the Summer of 1907 the architect was asked to show 'greater energy' so that contractors could get on and finish their work without scaffolding getting in the way.

Even after the Service of Rededication on St Andrews Day 1909 there were matters yet to be resolved, proposals agreed, and decisions made. In particular designs for stained glass windows had to be approved. The great Te Deum east window by Douglas Strachan, the three north transept windows by James Powell and Sons, and the windows on either side of the south porch, also by James Powell and Sons, had already been agreed. Before the Committees were disbanded in December 1911, further proposals for stained glass windows were approved – the east window of the north aisle, which contained the only glass from the old church, by Messrs Ballantine and Sons,

Edinburgh; the Hunter chapel windows by Louis Davis; the east window in the south aisle, the Miracles of Christ by Douglas Strachan in memory of Stuart Grace, father of C.S. Grace, and of his wife Jessie Playfair; and the window by the tower door by Douglas Strachan. The main window in the south transept by Reginald Hallward caused considerable anxiety. The design required some modification, but a more serious problem had to be overcome as the Inland Revenue claimed duty on the £1,000 legacy of Miss Beatrice Broughton. In the end all was well as her niece paid an extra £100 at the time of dedication. Of course after the handing over of the building further stained glass windows were installed, some by Douglas Strachan, for example the great west window donated by the women of the congregation, and the clerestorey windows by his brother Alexander in memory of those who were killed in World War I. Ronald Cant writes: 'By great good fortune the restoration coincided with one of the finest periods in the revival of stained glass, Douglas Strachan's carefully contrasting designs for the eastward and westward vistas of the central nave being of particularly outstanding merit.' Holy Trinity is a treasure house of twentieth-century stained glass.

The final architect's account – he was criticised in October 1910 for delay – was presented to the Executive Committee in February 1911. After much wrangling the accounts were agreed and the shortfall of £2,011.2s.8d made up. At the penultimate meeting of the General Committee on December 28th, 1911 with Dr Playfair in the chair the accounts were approved and the Heritors were deemed to take over the building the next day. This duly happened and, before disbanding, the General Committee received a final report that 'the Heritors had, at a meeting to-day, taken over from this Committee as from the present time the Building of the Church together with the Stained Glass Windows therein and had discharged the Committee of all further liability in connection with the Restoration of the Church'.

Responsibility now lies with the General Trustees of the Church of Scotland and the Congregational Board of Holy Trinity.

Expressions of gratitude and thanks for the work of the two principal leaders of the project, Dr Playfair and Mr C.S.Grace, were given at a public dinner on March 28th, 1911 in the Town Hall with Sir Ralph Anstruther in the Chair. A presentation to Dr Playfair was made by Sheriff Armour-Hannay, whose daughter Marjory was later to marry Dr Playfair's son Jack. An inscription in Latin by Professor Herkless over the entrance to the church was approved by a meeting of the Sub-Committee in February 1910 while Dr Playfair was on holiday in Madeira on his doctor's advice. He playfully referred to it as 'the surreptitious stone'. It reads in translation: 'This Parish Church dedicated AD 1412 in the name of the Holy Trinity, was restored in the year of salvation 1909 to its former dignity, Patrick Macdonald Playfair, D.D., being Minister of the First Charge and himself leader of the work, Peter MacGregor Chalmers having been called to counsel as Architect.' For both men it was the fulfilment of a dream.

The Last Supper

Luke XXII 15: With desire I have desired to eat this passover with you before I suffer.

There must have been in the Saviour's mind a sense of relief that a weary life was well nigh over. You have seen poor sufferers earnestly longing for the coming of the last summons; you have seen disappointed, heart-broken, bereaved ones longing to meet the hour when the frail thread binding them to this life should be severed and the released soul wing its flight to the land of reunion and eternal peace. Jesus must have longed for the end of his toil and sorrow. Was not this the hour of which He once said: "Mine hour is not yet come"? Was it not to this night that He had been looking forward all His life working so strenuously that He might be ready for it?

Doubtless it was pleasant for Him to spend a peaceful hour in the society of souls who were of a kindred spirit, away from the turmoil of a hostile world. There had not been many such hours during the three crowded years of His ministry and to hold communion with those who loved Him at this crisis would be consoling and even strengthening. Has it ever been yours to have to go through some great parting? Has it ever been yours to leave familiar scenes and loving friends? If so, you may possibly recall sadly peaceful hours when for the last time you looked on the familiar objects, visited the old scene and performed the oft told task. You may recollect the last evening you spent, the last hour, the last words you spoke to well-tried friends; the last grasp of the strong hand that silently expressed so fervent a God-speed; the last moment you heard the well-known voices ere the turn of the road cut them off. And there are other partings when we remain behind and others leave – leave for the battlefield of life, leave for the long journey for the land which is very far off. It is at such times that depths of love and tenderness are discovered in hearts till then unfathomed. We look back on them with sad pleasure. The words of thanks, of sweet praise are ever with us.

Were there not then thoughts of such things in our Master's mind which induced Him to desire to eat that last supper with His little circle of friends that they might remember the blessed hours? Christ would not have been mortal and the loving Friend He was had He not had some such feelings.

Then too He longed that at last He might be able to seal with His blood the new covenant of grace and truth and to proclaim from the Cross His boundless love and the freedom from condemnation of all who might believe in and follow Him. To His death He looked not as the end of and release from His work but as the central point in it. On the Cross He was to influence men: 'And I, if I be lifted up on high, shall draw all men unto me.' All that sorrow, pain and death could wreak upon Him He was ready to endure that men might go free. As the million lights of star-land pale and the moon hides her borrowed rays before the glory of the morning sun so, Christ knew, would all shadows and types of sacrifice offered up through the long, weary night of expectation vanish from before the one great sacrifice offered on the Cross; all distinction between Jew and Gentile would cease; and the fulfillment of all the prophecies of better days in store for the nations as they turned to serve the true God would commence. And He knew that by entering Jerusalem that night to keep the feast He was placing Himself in the power of those who would not scruple to take advantage of His presence to compass His death and so, unwittingly, to inaugurate the true golden age of the world. Could He then, whose heart beat in sympathy with every prisoner to evil, every oppressed people, everyone lost in the darkness and blinded by error, fail to welcome the event which was to bring to Him His soul's desire? Must it not indeed have needed an intense heroism, a most marvellous and transcendent patience to go on slowly educating His disciples and unfolding to them His plans while He saw that world which He came to deliver lying still in darkness! If we have set our hearts on any special object how apt we are to chafe and fret at all which hinders us from attaining it! It was not so indeed in Jesus's case for patience and self-control were in Him no less than manly energy and steadfast resolve. Yet we can well believe that the very strain of the constant exercise of patience would heat to the burning point the desire for the end. And we can well understand how as each day passed away His heart would be filled with a greater joy and an ever-growing yearning.

And yet again He desired to eat this Passover because He longed to institute that holy feast which brings to His beloved followers peace and power. Long had He thought of this. It was not enough that He was to give His life for men, it was not enough that He should leave His kingdom, His glory, and His eternal joy, to become poor, outcast and abased for men – His love would carry Him further and He would leave them a legacy which might perpetually remind them of His love and His work. He had compassion on men because they were like ships out in the night of life's stormy sea wandering amidst hardship and perils and He gave them the guiding light of truth to bring them home. He had compassion on them also because He saw how they were toiling on, faint and scarce able to persevere, therefore He would give them wells of water in the valley of weeping and would spread a table for them in the presence of their enemies. He desired to see all men gathered round Him. He saw a prophecy and a beginning in the Passover. Surely then we should attach supreme importance to this feast! Is there not in the disclosure of this intense desire a reply to those who would make the Lord's Supper a mere outward observance, nothing more than the commemoration of a good man!

Do these words not lend solemnity to His every syllable and action in this Feast which is to be perpetuated from that night to the end? Is not this legacy of surpassing love a Sacrament – an exhibition of divine promises showing forth to us His loving kindness and His willingness to give us of Himself? There must be some object, some person, to nourish love. The divine love of Christ bursts all bonds and passes in life-giving streams over all mankind. In the Sacrament He has given to His followers a manifestation of that love. With desire He desired to eat that Passover that men might be continually reminded of His love.

Christ has passed from earth but still He desires to meet with His people at His table. Does this marvellous condescension make no appeal to us? Does it not rebuke our slowness of heart, the perfunctoriness of much of our service and obedience? It is strange that He should allow us to commune with Him after the manner of the chosen twelve but with far less excuse, we who have so often played Him false and murmured against Him. But that He should desire to receive us, that He should stretch out His arms to enfold us, that He should beckon and call us as we wander away from Him or stand coldly aloof – all this is a mystery beyond our comprehension!

Christ desires to eat with us. How shall we escape danger, sin and woe if we neglect that desire? "All day long have I stretched out my hands," He cries, "ye would not come to me that ye might have life." Is anything hidden from Him? Does He not know all our sinfulness? And yet He desires to meet us that we might be cleansed, changed and sanctified. Let it be ours to accept His invitation in all humility, to listen to His gracious words, and to receive His offered help.

This sermon was first preached in Glencairn on June 19th, 1887, and later in St Michael's, Dumfries, in October 1897, at St Andrews in St Mary's in August 1906 and in Holy Trinity in November 1912, in Rutger's Presbyterian Church, New York in October 1913, and in Elie in October 1914.

Christ as the Solid Foundation

I Corinthians III 11–15: For other foundation can no man lay than that is laid, which is Jesus Christ. Now if any man build on this foundation gold, silver, precious stones, wood, hay, stubble; every man's work shall be made manifest: for the day shall declare it, because it shall be revealed by fire; and the fire shall try every man's work of what sort it is. If any man's work abide which he hath built thereupon, he shall receive a reward. If any man's work shall be burned, he shall suffer loss: but he himself shall be saved; yet so as by fire.

One foundation but many builders. In these words is summed up the story of the erection of many of the most venerable and imposing structures in our land. The foundation was the work of one designer. Piece by piece the superstructure was added. Then came the time of trial. Storm, fire and the ruthless hands of short-sighted men did their worst. Cathedral, church and castle illustrate our text. Wherever that true and good foundation was laid there we have still the root of the building, though much or all of the super-structure may have gone.

St Paul speaks of foundation, superstructure and builders. He compares the Church of Christ to a building and Christ's servants to the builders. It is of the Church of Christ universal and indivisible that he speaks. The foundation is Christ. That foundation is already laid and no other can be laid. Paul has the privilege of pointing out to the nations this sure foundation, he may show men how to build thereon but the foundation is already there, Christ Himself. Remove

Christ and His Church must fall to pieces. No system of doctrine or church government can uphold the fabric of the Church. On Christ alone can we rest. There is much for Paul and Christ's ministers and people to do, but the only essential groundwork is prepared for them.

The foundation is *one*, being Christ; the building is one, being His universal Church; but the builders are many and the materials they use are various. Some build at one point and some at another; some in one age, some in another; some build with care and strongly, others without thought and weakly; some use in their work gold, silver and precious stones, some build with wood, hay and stubble – configuration and appearance may be the same but the materials and the labour involved differ.

But our text tells us of a coming day when all the labours of the different workers will be subjected to searching trial – when all that is right, the gold, silver and precious stones shall abide and the builder be rewarded, when all that is wrong, the wood, hay and stubble shall be burned and the builder suffer loss. *Certain kinds of work will be destroyed.*

The trial of every man's work is to be by the fire of judgement. It is suggested that the Apostle employed this language when writing to the Corinthians because of some recent great fire in their city where all the less substantial houses were destroyed and only the stately temples remained to tell of the former grandeur of the whole. In the day of judgement only the work of those who have preached and taught Christ crucifed and have walked in His steps will stand, while all labour which has had for its tendancy the glorification of human effort and the neglect of Christ Himself shall fall in pieces.

Still, let us make no mistake here. These unworthy materials, this unsubstantial work, are all *part of the building* of which Christ is the foundation. Within the Church there is too much work which has as little chance of enduring as wood or straw. There are some who preach

Christ in a spirit of contention and bitterness far removed from the Master's example. There are some who forget that the building should harmonise with the foundation – who seem to forget Christ while they preach Christianity, who through a mistaken charity would deceive those building on other foundations into believing that they too are building on Christ. And there are some also who would require of their followers *more* than Christ demands. It is such teaching as this which is unenduring work.

They labour for naught. *They* get no reward for their work; but, more than that, they shall see that portion of the structure which they so toilsomely erected, crumble into dust before their eyes. They shall find that theological and ecclesiastical strife is not religion, that unholy, envious rivalry is not zeal in God's service, that bigotry is not purity, that breadth is not necessarily charity, that eccentricities and vagaries do not ornament but disfigure that building whose grandeur lies in simplicity and whose beauty is only found in purity.

But, *though the works of some perish still the builders are saved*. The worker has passed through extreme peril – his *life* is saved, nothing more. It is like the case of a man who has been through long years labouring in some distant land till at last having gathered together enough to last him to the end of life, he takes his passage home carrying with him all his treasure. But before he reaches port a raging storm flings his vessel on the hidden reef and the towering waves scatter it and its cargo on all sides and engulf it in their waters; only the passengers and crew are saved by the lifeboat. All his goods have perished; he himself is saved. Or it is like some man awakened in the night time by the dread cry of 'Fire'. He is hurried through the smoke and flames to the escape and his life is saved, but his house and all it contained are reduced to ashes. The man who builds with wood and straw in Christ's Church saves his life but naught else.

He who built with hay is saved just as he is who built with gold

– but the one is saved and *no more*, the other is saved, his work abides, he receives reward. In heaven there is no equality as we use the word. God does not judge with the imperfect knowledge and justice of man. Not of necessity will they be nearest to Him hereafter who have occupied uppermost seats on earth. But they who most truly showed faith in Christ in word and life shall shine most brightly in the kingdom of the Father.

Many builders and one building. Shall we not recognise here a plea for tolerance? Even those who build with the more enduring materials do not all build with the same. All do not use precious stones and gold. Others may work in a different way from us and yet be as good or better builders. It is more important for us to examine our own work to see that it is not squandered on the things that perish than to criticise and carp at something in others which offends our too delicate senses. We builders must work with all our might and with all our mind lest our own labours go for naught and we blemish or retard the building of the Church of Christ as, alas! so many do.

It is sad for the man who has toiled for a whole year when harvest comes to have to return home without a single sheaf leaving all rotting in the field; sad if it be through adverse circumstances, sadder far if it be through his own fault. But what will such sadness be compared with that of the man who has spent all his life, knowing Christ, in His Church yet wasting his whole strength in trying to build up a Christian life with wood, hay or stubble.

Let us labour then that our life, and the Church of Christ so far as we are concerned, may be built of solid, sound, enduring masonry. It is a great thing to have a sure foundation. We *have* that. That foundation is *enough, if* we can do no more than cling to it – but it is not enough if we *can* do more. In Norway where wood is plentiful and building stone scarce many of the houses are built of wood but always there is a foundation and a course or two of stone. If we have no material at hand but wood we must do the best we can with it, but if we can do better we must not be content with what will perish when fire comes to try it. And if we build faithfully on the true foundation with the right material, our work will never be unfinished. It may be only the merest fragment which has risen into shape under our hands but it has and retains its place in the building.

This sermon was first preached in Glencairn in February 1888, and later at St Andrews in St Mary's in November 1903 and in Holy Trinity in August 1924.

Portrait of the Revd Dr Patrick Macdonald Playfair by Douglas Strachan painted in 1911.

Courtesy of St Andrews University Museum Collections

The Town Kirk today

Gargoyle

Two gargoyles

Stone carving.
Two cherubs symbolizing
Prayer

Stone carving.
The Burning Bush,
symbol of the Church
of Scotland, with the
date of the
Rededication 1909.

Interior of church today

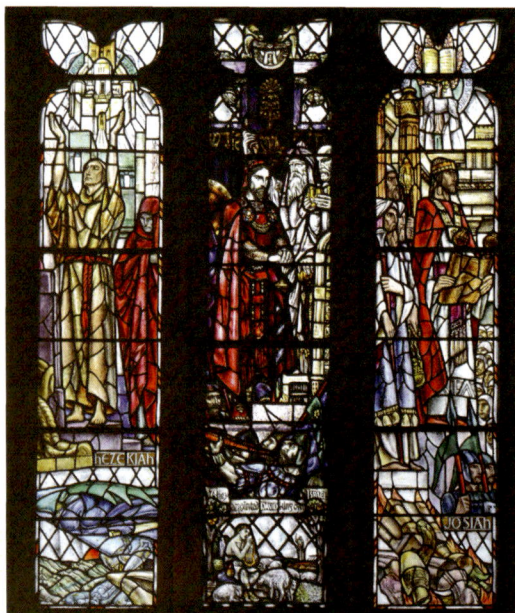

Three Old Testament Kings.

A stained glass window by Douglas Strachan, the right light in memory of Dr and Mrs Patrick Playfair

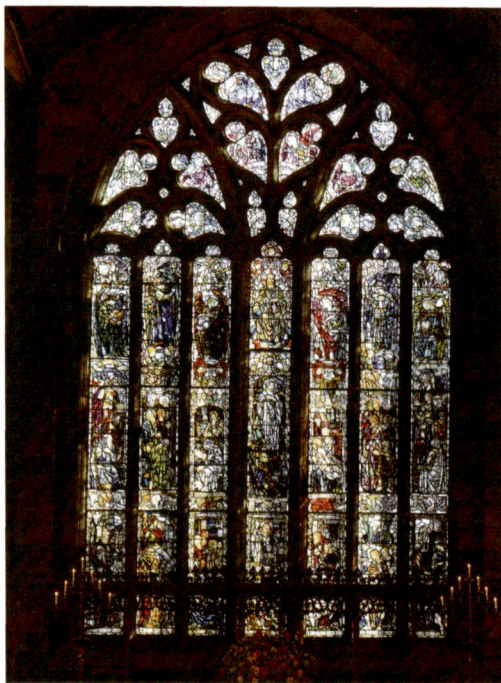

The Great East Window by Douglas Strachan

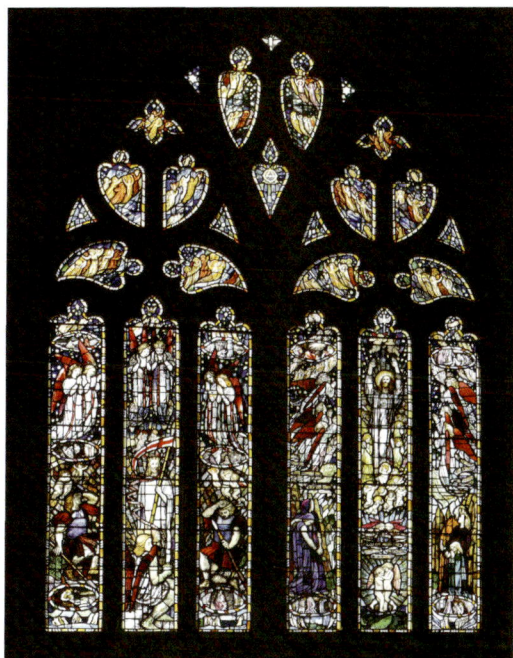

The South Transept Window by Reginald Hallward

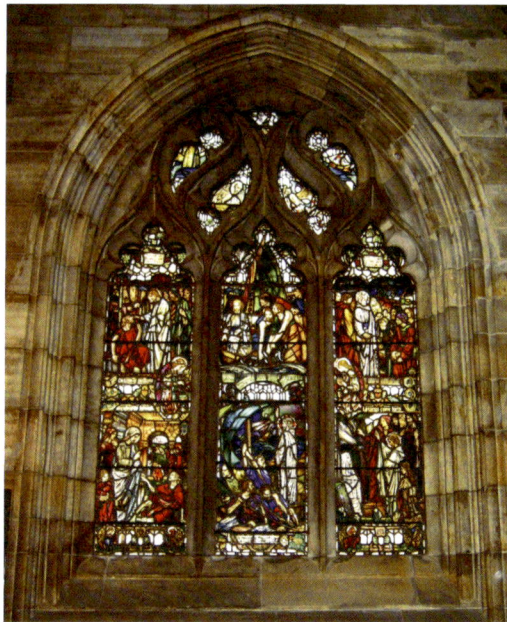

Six Miracles of Christ.

A stained glass window by Douglas Strachan, the subject of Dr Patrick Playfair's sermon preached at the Dedication on January 8th, 1911

Stone carving.
The Good Shepherd with children's heads

Stone carving.
The Parable of the Drag Net

Font in memory of Dr A.K.H. Boyd

Communion Table
In memory of all who have ministered and worshipped in this place

*The pulpit of Iona marble, alabaster and onyx in memory
of Dr A.K.H. Boyd, Minister of the First Charge 1865–99*

*Dove with olive branch
above the pulpit,
formerly on top of the
sounding board of the
pulpit in the nineteenth
century church*

Carved wooden angels in the Hunter Memorial Chapel

The Sharp Monument in the South Transept
as in the nineteenth century church

Hour Glass, which belonged to Dr Patrick Playfair

Token to commemorate the Rededication of the Parish Church,
St Andrews on St Andrew's Day 1909

The Mystery of the Trinity

Matthew XXVIII 19: In the name of the Father, and of the Son, and of the Holy Ghost.

There are seasons when our thoughts are directly turned to God the Father, others when we think more of God the Son, and still others when the Holy Ghost is chiefly in our minds. There are movements in the Church which have as their object concentration upon the Almighty Ruler of the Universe, or upon Jesus Christ the Redeemer of Mankind, or upon the life-giving, sanctifying Spirit. The love of God, if it is to be known, must be known as revealed in the Father, the Son and the Holy Ghost.

But we must not forget to consider also that these three Persons are only one God, that they are 'the same in substance, equal in power and glory'.

The doctrine of the Trinity is one of the mysteries of Christianity. There are familiar facts of daily experience, many of the surest discoveries and deductions of natural science, which, though perfectly intelligible and capable of being rationally believed and demonstrably established, are yet in a high degree mysterious. Yet there is nothing known to us analogous to this doctrine of the Trinity.

Scripture teaches us that the Father, the Son, and the Holy Spirit are not merely powers or activities of the nature of God; they are distinctions in the Divine nature expressing not aspects of that nature but each expressing by itself the entire essence. Through each Person at the same time and in the same degree the whole of God, the whole of love, is revealed, though in a different way. All the Divine attributes are in the Father who created the world by His divine Word. All the Divine attributes are in the Son, the eternal Word who was in the beginning with God, and was Himself God, through whom all things are created, and who when the time was fulfilled was made Flesh and dwelt among men. All the Divine attributes are in the Holy Spirit through whom we know what is given us by God.

Yet while we may understand these facts mystery underlies them. We cannot find out the Almighty unto perfection. Nevertheless the logic of the intellect is transcended by that of the heart. We ponder the Trinity not that our *reason* but that our *heart* may grasp the doctrine. 'The good man that feels the power of the Father and to whom the Son has become wisdom and righteousness, and in whom the love of the Spirit is spread; this man alone understands the mystery of the Trinity. In this case experience is the best learning, and Christianity is the best institution, and the Spirit of God is the best teacher and holiness is the greatest wisdom, and he that sins most is the most ignorant, and the humble and obedient man is the best scholar.'

Is it true that apart from this doctrine of the Trinity we cannot know God as He would have us know Him? If it is surely we will find testimony in the Holy Scriptures. Do we not find there the Father addressing the Son as 'Thou', and the Son addressing the Father in like manner? 'That they may all be one, as Thou, Father, art in Me and I in Thee.' Then both Father and Son are represented as speaking of the Holy Spirit as 'He' or 'Him'. 'But the Comforter which is the Holy Ghost whom the Father will send in My name, He shall teach you all things.' The Father is said to give the Son and to send Him into the world. 'God so loved the world that He gave His only-begotten Son.' 'God sent the Son into the world not to condemn the world.' The Son undertakes the Father's work and 'comes to do not His own will, but the will of the Father that sent Him'. The Son was in the bosom of the Father and had glory with the Father before the world was. The Spirit again is spoken of by the Son as 'another Comforter'. He is to be sent by the Son from the

Father. He proceeds from the Father and testifies of the Son and through the Son we both (Jews and Gentiles) have access by one Spirit unto the Father.

From these and similar passages it seems clear that Scripture at least speaks of three Persons – not three aspects of one Person. Do not let us pass over a matter such as this because it is difficult. The fact that this doctrine is 'full of mystery and overruns with questions before which the mind stands helpless is not an objection to its truth, but it is rather what man ought to look for in any revelation which proceeds from God'. Do not let us be carried away by the idea that creed is immaterial as conduct alone counts. Creed influences conduct that is to say *real creed* – belief in the *heart*. For creed is not the saying of 'Lord, Lord', it is believing in the heart that God *is* Lord. Creed is not the mere statement that Jesus Christ is the Redeemer of the world, it is the realising in the heart that He is *our* Redeemer. Where there is sincere belief in the existence of God the Father, that Christ is our Saviour and that the Holy Spirit can guide us in the way of life and purify us from evil the conduct *must* be influenced. It is the creed of the lips only that is powerless for good. Too often the Son and the Holy Ghost have assigned to their position and power less than Divine. Jesus Christ is a mere man who raised himself to the highest degree of resemblance to God the world has yet seen – the greatest so far of all the prophets and teachers. The Holy Ghost is a force or activity – not God Himself – who dwells in His Church.

If these views are right Holy Scripture does not seem to be a safe guide in this matter, and Christianity is no perfect revelation, for God alone is able to reveal the Almighty as He is. And as God can only be revealed through Himself so can He only be loved and appropriated through Himself.

Scripture never presents us with mystery without good purpose. If there had been no gain for us in this doctrine it would not have been revealed. If the world could have done as well without as with it silence would have been observed.

Creed is intended to influence conduct but men often say 'I believe' when they do not. We must not confuse profession with confession. Every professor of Christianity is by no means a confessor.

The doctrine of the Trinity teaches that God is not an inanimate idol 'a stream of tendency flowing through the ages' but our Father in heaven with an ear ever open to prayer, a heart full of sympathy and an arm mighty to save; that the Son is not merely an example we *may* follow but one we *must*, not a guide to salvation but Himself a Saviour; that the Spirit is not a subtle emanation from God but Himself God acting not from an infinite distance but within us.

Believe these things in your heart and your conduct cannot fail to be pleasing to God. 'Be sure that it is only by complete willingness to know His completest truth that we can rightly know anything regarding God's surpassing nature.' Ponder them well that in your heart and in your homes there be no altar erected to an unknown God.

This sermon was first preached in Glencairn on May 28th, 1893, and later at St Andrews in Holy Trinity in May 1907 and in St Mary's in June 1911.

Paul and the Kingdom of God

Acts XXVIII 30–31: And Paul dwelt two whole years in his own hired house, and received all that came in unto him, preaching the kingdom of God, and teaching those things which concern the Lord Jesus Christ, with all confidence, no man forbidding him.

It would have been deeply interesting if St Luke had continued his narrative and gone on to tell something of the captivity endured by St Paul. But for some reason this is the last verse of the Acts of the Apostles. We learn however from the Epistles that chains could not bind the spirit, curb the zeal or fetter the tongue of the great Apostle. He used his very adversity for the good of his cause; his house of bondage became a temple where many found freedom. The prisoner, patient, kind and forgiving, overcame the prejudice and coarse contempt of his guards. One by one they came under the power of the Gospel he preached, till the finest body of troops in the Roman army was leavened with Christianity; till his bonds and the truths he taught were the subject of conversation throughout the mistress city of the world; till there were saints even in Caesar's household.

This is the last word of St Luke concerning that beloved friend. And a most striking word it is – in fullest harmony with all which he had already written about St Paul and yet, if possible, showing an even more intense devotion on the part of this famous man to his great mission. It dwells in our memory as a marvellous example of courage, constancy and love. Never does St Paul appear greater than he does when, physically weak, galled by his chains and the intolerable presence of his guard, uncertain as to the direction of his imprisonment, and doubtful as to the results of his trial, he deliberately sets himself to make his lodgings a beacon-light in that evil city whose sun had far passed the zenith.

But our imagination carries us away from his narrow lodgings, away from the Eternal City out into the whole Roman world. What do we see there? Released prisoners bearing to their own peoples the things concerning Christ; slaves carrying to their new homes words of eternal hope for themselves and their fellows, even for their masters and mistresses; soldiers who had kept vigil beside the intrepid captive telling over the camp fire in many a land the glad tidings of great joy they had found through his bold, earnest words. More and more heard the message issuing day by day during those two whole years from the Apostle's lodgings. More and more believed as they saw the peasant leading a purer life, the slave rendering better service, the soldier facing death with greater fearlessness because of the Gospel.

We too are Christians and it lies on us as it lay on him to preach the Kingdom of God. What is the Kingdom of God?

There are round about us structures and organisations which are outward professions of its presence; there are schemes of men who would use Christianity to hold nations in subjection and despoil the people – these are *not* the Kingdom of God. There is in the guise of religion an unholy strife and contention for supremacy among men but the Kingdom of God is not in such bitter rivalry and confusion. There are the manifest, restless movements of sectarian zealots; there are the plots and counterplots among the Churches – but the Kingdom of God is outside all such things. Men may think to spread God's Kingdom by the bustle and excitement of new devices and enterprises continually conceived – but God's Kingdom, like God Himself, is not in the noisy, cumbrous forms of human societies. It is a strangely silent power. It came into the world while men slept. Long expected signs came not. It exists as silently as it was born; it exists for any man in his heart; in his character, thoughts, acts and affections. 'The

Kingdom of God is *within* you.' It is the obedience of the unseen spirit of man to the unseen Lord of all. If you are citizens of the Kingdom of God you are not content with belonging to this or that Church, with professing this or that creed, with performing these or those ceremonies, with joining this or that movement or organization; but you are living under the power of God's Spirit, you are seeking that your whole life shall be moulded by that Power. And what is the Kingdom of God but just the aggregate of all such humble, thirsting, striving, believing souls?

This Kingdom is an affair of the soul, of moral power. It is necessary to remind ourselves of this for we live in an age of steel, steam and electricity, an age which boasts of its mechanical skill and its ingenuity for contriving the means of superseding the necessity for man's effort and of its little victories over earth and sea and air. And the tendency of the age is felt too in the Christian Church, where we see on many sides the effort made to extend the Kingdom's influence by superficial machinery and external impetus, and to measure its growth by a wealth of figures, instead of by the power of lives submissive to and filled with the Holy Ghost.

Outward organisation may be most advisable but what is *essential* is inward life. We are to preach the Kingdom of God and we cannot preach it unless we are *in* it. 'The secret of the Lord is with them that fear Him', and the secret of His Kingdom is revealed only to its citizens – neither natural wisdom nor material strength can wrest to itself the knowledge and power thereof. It is by the silent strength of a consistent, holy life that we will know and impress on men its reality and power, by a steady life of faith and purity, by the conquest of temper and lust.

We turn to other words by our Apostle. 'The Kingdom of God is not meat and drink, but righteousness and peace and joy in the Holy Ghost'. It does not consist in forms and ceremonies and the observance of a whole multitude of rites and garbs, but something far more practical and vital – *righteousness, peace and joy. There* is reality with no possibility of deceit. I go into a magnificent cathedral, its walls coloured by the light streaming through its gorgeous windows, a great spectacle is spread before me, priests arrayed in magnificent garments, crowds of worshippers sway to the sound of silver bells, majestic music falls upon my ear – and I am bewildered. What does it mean? Is it a splendid jewelled casket holding nothing? Or is it the outward expression of the superabounding spiritual life of the worshippers? I cannot tell – God knows. But full of perplexity I go out to the street and there, amidst a throng of pleasure seekers on that Sunday morning, I see a young, fragile looking, beautiful woman slowly pacing along supporting an aged, half-paralytic friend, crabbed, grumbling and ungrateful. No envious glance does she throw on others who hurry past her, no blush of shame mantles her cheek, no look of aversion or martyrdom to duty crosses her shapely features; but with an unruffled, smiling face she tries to interest the old man in objects at their side and to infuse into him a little of her tranquility. And I think: 'Thank God, this at least can be no pretence or mere form.' I know that the Kingdom of God is *there*. 'By their fruits ye shall know them.'

The Kingdom of God is *rightness and justice* – the loving of what is right is the sign of its existence within us. If we are unjust and lovers of wrongdoing we are not in the Kingdom and we cannot preach it. Cheating, oppression, uncharitableness, injustice, greed, drunkenness, impurity – these cannot be found in the same soul as the Kingdom. It is impossible. No man can serve two masters. The Kingdom of God makes us righteous if we receive it and submit to its power; it makes us lovers and doers of what is right; it makes us preachers of *righteousness* to our fellow men.

Peace is another sign of the Kingdom. 'We complain,' writes a well known author, 'of the want of many things; we want votes, we want liberty, we want amusements, we want money – which of us feels he wants peace?' 'I know,' wrote Charles Kingsley, 'that what we all want is inward rest – rest of heart and brain, the calm, strong, self-contained, self-denying character which needs no stimulants for it has no fits of depression; which needs no narcotics for it has no fits of excitement; which needs no ascetic restraints for it is strong enough to use God's gifts without abusing them.' We need peace and peace comes when the Kingdom comes into the heart. It comes in its own time. You do not learn to do justly in a day; nor can you all at once have the peace of God ruling in your hearts. Keep from out of your heart pride and avarice, selfishness and ambition, hatred and injustice which disturb and sully its purity and you will have peace. Your life stream will run clear and full and your peace will overflow into the lives of others. You will be truly preachers of *peace* to your fellow men.

There remains the third sign of the Kingdom – *joy*. We all wish happiness. Many seek it in the wrong way. Solomon sought it in pleasure and ruined his kingdom. Judas sought it in gold and silver, and found instead disease and death. Some, like Anthony, seek it in love and like him find disgrace. Others look for it in dominion, like Caesar, and find ingratitude. To have real joy, as to have peace we must cast evil out of our hearts, and we can only do so by turning them to God, as the flowers turn to the sun, and drinking in His life, by fixing our affections on Him and receiving and obeying His every command. Neither wealth nor rank, nor popularity, nor learning will secure joy – without rightness and peace you may be rich, powerful, fawned on, denizens of knowledge yet you cannot be truly happy. But accept the rule of the Kingdom of God – follow its spirit and your joy will be full, so full that it will be visible to all and you will be preachers of joy to your fellow men.

Remember then your duty to your own souls, to your fellow men, above all to God. Receive the Kingdom of God, obey it, have its blessings and, whatsoever your position or circumstances may be, even though they be adverse as those of Paul in Rome, you will through your lives be preachers to all of righteousness, peace and joy – preachers of the Kingdom of God.

This sermon was preached first in Glencairn on June 28th, 1896, and later in Holy Trinity, St Andrews in June 1899, in St Columba's, London in March 1903, and in Rutger's Presbyterian Church, New York in October 1913.

New Beginnings

Mark VI 48, 51: And he saw them toiling in rowing; for the wind was contrary unto them … and he went up unto them into the ship; and the wind ceased.

The disciples had enjoyed a brief time of rest, after which they had been sent away by Jesus down to the sea. He had 'constrained' them to go. Perhaps they went reluctantly for rest is pleasant and, fond though we may be of our work when we are at it, we often need to put some pressure on ourselves to resume it after an interval of relaxation. It is often easier to keep plodding on than to begin again after we have stopped. We have seen the poor horse struggling to bring into motion the heavy load which it kept moving with comparative ease when it was once started. So we often find it hard to make a new beginning.

It is not agreeable to embark on the sea when the signs all point, if not to rough weather, at least to constant strain and possible peril. Duty may constrain us to do it and it is well to give due consideration to the claims of duty. But, duty is such a cold, heartless and unbending director. It has neither love nor sympathy. So it is better to think of our work as set us by God our Father, who loves us with a love we cannot fathom and understands our fears and difficulties. It was Jesus who constrained His disciples to get into the ship.

The work involved is given us by God. 'What difference does it make if the work comes by accident or through God?' The difference is this – if it comes by accident it may be wrong; if it comes from God it must be right. It is easier and more pleasant to work for a father whom we love than merely to discharge a piece of duty. Love is a great incentive to work and a great lightener of labour. Furthermore, we work with far more confidence of success if we are convinced that God requires us to do what is set before us. We may not draw any distinction between God and duty for the one is the cause of the other. We must recognise the clear distinction between God and accident.

In what spirit are we to embark upon these new campaigns?

Firstly, with *courage*. Whatever the work, new or continuing, we must take our courage in our hands in any work. Our work is before us and it has to be done. If the winds prove favourable well and good; but if they be contrary we have just to face and fight them. It is a glorious sight to see the vessel with every stitch of canvas spread rushing before the following wind, spearing the waves and splitting their crests, and raising clouds of spray to glisten in the sunshine. But it cannot be always so. The wind may change or the ship must turn, and then every inch has to be fought for. It is no use grumbling – no amount of grumbling will alter the direction or force of the gale. We must fight it – resolute not to be overcome by adversity and alert to take advantage of every favourable circumstance. It is no use to wish we had not left the shore and we must not let danger foreseen keep us from starting, unless the task is clearly beyond our powers – then it is no disgrace and no desertion of duty to decline to start, or should we have started to turn back if we can, for there too is the guiding hand of God.

Nor should we forget that it is often in beating up against the wind that true worth is discovered. It is the struggle against difficulties which reveals resource and develops courage. There is no demand for these things when all goes well. The fishing disciples are a lesson to us all as we see them out in the darkness on the deep 'toiling in rowing'. They were learning from the great Master that difficulties are made to be overcome. So, when a sea of troubles threatens us let us 'take arms and by opposing end them'.

It is well to remember too that the brave encountering of difficulty makes us stronger and better men and women. When we have toiled in rowing we have not only shown our courage in meeting opposition but we have also gained experience, skill and confidence which stand us in good stead ever after. We know what we can do, and how to do it, and look to the future with a lighter heart.

Secondly, with *patience*. Our patience may be tried as well as our courage. We may be tempted to say: 'What is the good of going on, we have worked long and honestly and we are hardly making progress?' We toil and there seems to be no proportionate result. It takes so much time and strength to hold even the little we have. It is then that patience is called for – patience to remember that God has sent us out to work continually but not necessarily to make continual progress. We need patience to wait until the ebb is ended and the flow bears us on its swelling flood right up to the harbour. And the need for patience may be intensified when we see others progressing rapidly in the same work wherein we seem to be at a standstill. The scholar struggles with a lesson which a companion masters easily. The mother labours to bend a wayward child to obedience, truth and righteousness with so little apparent result while a neighbour's child has followed the better way, like Samuel, from early years. The teacher toils to instruct a backward class feeling that the labour is thrown away when compared with his more apt pupils. The preacher strives to guide others into safety and to overcome the evils of life and society, yet sees the wanderers and the fallen as numerous as ever, when a brother succeeds in turning many souls to God. All need patience to keep them from giving up their work and looking for a more promising task. Indeed, our Lord had His patience tried in His work. He saw very few results. Many flocked round, many listened to His words, and many went away with no commitment. His patience was sublime. Let us recall Sir Philip Sidney's words, 'Fortify courage with the true rampart of patience'.

Thirdly, with *hope*. Our Lord reaped little Himself yet the harvest has not been wanting. The disciples toiled in rowing but they were obeying their Master; they remembered how on a previous occasion He stilled the tempest and delivered them. They would have confident hope that now they would not toil in vain. None who do God's work labour in vain. In due season we reap the reward of our efforts. The lesson which seemed so hard to learn is learned; the difficulty overcome the way is made easy for a time. The wind is no longer contrary, the tide turns in our favour and we glide on. Much of our work is pleasant, exhilarating, and on the whole easy. We must not allow ourselves to follow the thoughts of those who continually groan over what they call the sorrows of their toil because it is always disagreeable and irksome. Much of it is quite the reverse and many are never so truly happy – indeed wise people are never so happy as when they are at work.

Let us strengthen patience and courage with hope. No task is hopeless to those who see that work and result must be considered together. Much work and little outcome may outweigh little work and great result as far as real merit and welfare are concerned. Let us see to it that we never put our mind and set our hand to anything that is unworthy of our labour and contrary to what we know to be the will of God.

One more point – the power of *sympathy*. We cannot overestimate the value of sympathy and yet too often we ignore it. What is more chilling and enfeebling than the feeling that those around us have no concern for our work and care not how we fare? What is more helpful than the kind enquiry, the hearty commendation, and the simple word of encouragement? We sometimes end a day profoundly depressed because so many have passed us by and never shown the smallest interest. But, thank God, many a time when things looked very black and we were nearly spent, a look, a word, an act of sympathy has acted like a charm. Let us remember that others need our sympathy just as we need theirs. They too may be strengthened by its presence or weakened by its absence. On that other occasion when Jesus was asleep in the storm tossed ship the cry of the fishermen was: 'Carest Thou not that we perish?' They were disheartened by the apparent want of sympathy for they thought, quite wrongly, that He did not care.

For many who are toiling hard and near to breaking point – known and unknown to us – our word, our look, our touch may make all the difference between defeat and success. We do not possess the might of the Son of God but often it is in our power to go up to a brother toiling away and bring him peace. Kindly sympathy extended to the toiler costs little and never comes amiss. We should never be above showing interest even in the little tasks of a child – his lessons, his difficulties, his perplexities. We should never laugh at his mistakes or ridicule his efforts. Nor should we shut our eyes to the great struggles of the wise and learned. They may be beyond our comprehension and outside our experience but we can at least learn. So we may have our share, through sympathy, in cheering someone in his labour and thus the world may be the richer merely because we looked with kindly, brotherly goodwill.

Finally, in our work let us take Christ as our example and seek from Him inspiration. But if we are truly to know Him we must kneel before Him in lowly reverence and fix our eyes upon Him with steadfast upward gaze. Many fail to see in Christ a reason to desire Him. It is because the humble heart and the upward look are lacking. The passing glance is not enough. He reveals Himself to the heart which longs, loves, thinks, and prays. And when the revelation comes there comes with it courage, patience, hope, and sympathy with our fellow men and women; for we become like Him when we see Him as He is.

This sermon was first preached on October 6th, 1901 in St Mary's, St Andrews, and later in Hope Park United Free Church, St Andrews in October 1904, in Holy Trinity, St Andrews in December 1912, Rutger's Presbyterian Church, New York in November 1913, and when introducing new Ministers to Inveresk in May 1906, Braemar in April 1907, Yarrow in November 1912, and Stranraer in December 1915. It was obviously quite a favourite.

The Cost of Discipleship

Luke XIV 27–30: And whosoever doth not bear his cross, and come after me, cannot be my disciple. For which of you, intending to build a tower, sitteth not down first, and counteth the cost, whether he have sufficient to finish it? Lest haply, after he hath laid the foundation, and is not able to finish it, all that behold it begin to mock him, saying, This man began to build, and was not able to finish.

Some speak as if such words were not for practical guidance. Jesus had no object to serve by giving His hearers too dark a representation of discipleship. Why should He exaggerate its difficulty? Why should He repel men? We hear much these days about making Christianity easy for people and not asking too much of them. We are told that we should be content if men are moderately moral and not frighten them from religion altogether. But Jesus knew that His cause would never spread if supported by half-hearted, lukewarm disciples. We will never make others believe if we do not believe ourselves. We will never do much for a cause if we are not enthusiastic. If we deem it of so little value that we will not give up anything, if need be everything, for it we will only hinder its advance.

But as we think of all that complete devotion to Christ's cause may mean – the severance of earthly ties, the leaving of dearest friends, the giving up of life not through fire or by sword but perhaps through incessant toil and manifold privations – we may well shrink from so exacting a prospect. We are perhaps afraid of beginning a task we cannot finish. We are right to be afraid. No one is more justly held in contempt than the man on whom no reliance can be placed, who does not fulfil engagements and allows every trifle to turn him aside from duty.

But surely there is some other course open to us than that of beginning only to fail or of standing aloof altogether. We must all feel ourselves unequal to the task – surely we are not therefore to make no attempt. Christ did not mean that if we feel doubtful we should not even try to be His disciples.

The point He wishes to impress on us is the need to be of the right frame of mind. To rush headlong into any undertaking is foolish. To rush headlong into following Christ is foolish. Remember – He does not require us to be certain of success before entering upon some course of action, but He does urge us not to be thoughtless. A cause is seldom benefited by those who join it without reflection, who are drawn into some current of popular feeling, or carried away in some moment of emotion without any profound consideration and weighing up of the duty it requires and the sacrifices it demands. Those who act in such a way may at the time be perfectly sincere but the chances are that before long they are in danger of having to draw back, or to continue to occupy a position wherein they have lost all real interest. No doubt some may act in haste and in a way which after reflection seems more and more right, but the danger of the reverse is great. Have you considered those words in Jesus' explanation of the Parable of the Sower about the seed which fell in stony places 'straightway with joy receiveth it'? Is there not a suggestion of impulsive, thoughtless action and failure to count the cost? Is the Master not teaching us that joy is not enough to support us through the trials of a life devoted to Him? There must be a firmer foundation. There is much in Christ's teaching to attract – forgiveness and eternal life are welcome thoughts to all weary and heavy laden souls. There is much to give joy. But if Christianity is to be for us what we know it has been to Christ's true servants of old, we must have opened out our hearts to it and laid bare our life to its demands.

Now it is impossible for anyone to reckon up his resources and to feel justified in entering Christ's discipleship unless faith is given some part in the estimate. Well we may ask: 'Who is sufficient for these things?' But with humble confidence we may also answer with the thought: 'I can do all things through Christ which strengtheneth me.' We are entitled to count divine help amongst our resources. All things are possible to him who believes. Without the belief that he can look to God for help how can any man enter Christ's discipleship? To discover our need for faith is the first step and to make sure that faith is in our armoury is the second step towards success. "Believe and you will conquer," said the Italian patriot. To enter the Christian life without a sincere belief that God will help us is to court failure. If so we are trying to do what Jesus Himself did not dare to try. We cannot meet and overcome the innumerable temptations and difficulties of life unless persistently seeking help from outside ourselves. The cost of discipleship is far too great if we count only on our own determination, never too great if we include the help of God.

'Well, this following of Jesus is too hard for me and I will not attempt it – better not to begin than to begin and stop.' No one is justified in saying that, for it is not like building a tower where resources are limited – in the Christian life there is no limitation. It is not too hard if we have the will and the faith. It has not been too hard for many far worse situated than we are. There are many who find it possible to give up all for Jesus' sake. Count the cost not to throw up the whole thing in despair but to look round for help and be guided to the source of all power and might.

Many have laid down their lives, or ruined their health, or parted with their possessions for the good of others. They felt a call and were not turned aside from their purpose by the cost. They did not see how the end was to be attained, but they believed in the goodness of their cause. They had faith that God would not let them fail, and they were right. If it had been a question of their own resources they could not have begun their work, but they looked above them in faith and prayer and their handful of meal grew in a miraculous way keeping pace with the increased demands of their increased work. I think of Dr Barnardo and of General Booth. They did not start their schemes without sitting down and counting the cost and they reckoned rightly on their power of faith and prayer.

If God puts it into our hearts to build some tower for His glory and the welfare of mankind, so long as we are true to His inspiration and we thoughtfully and prayerfully set ourselves to that task, success will in time be ours.

> 'Be bounteous in thy faith, for not mis-spent
> Is confidence unto the Father lent;
> Thy need is sown and rooted for His rain ....
> Work on! One day beyond all thought of praise
> A sunny joy will crown thee with its rays
> Nor other than thy need thy recompense.'

This sermon was first preached in St Mary's, St Andrews on May 11th, 1902 and later in Holy Trinity, St Andrews in April 1906, in November 1917, and in September 1924.

Solomon's Prayer for Wisdom

I Kings III 9: Give therefore thy servant an understanding heart to judge thy people, that I may discern between good and bad.

Solomon did not ask God for more knowledge. Knowledge and wisdom are different things.

Knowledge itself is worth little. To learn all we can is a duty. God has not given us the opportunity of learning that we may neglect it. School is not to be looked upon as a burden by the young. Knowledge is not to be regarded as an unnecessary accomplishment. Young or old, let us strive to know as much as possible. Let us read the page of history and the book of nature. Let us walk about the world with our eyes open and see how God works in all Creation, and we will learn about Him day by day.

But knowledge is very different from and inferior to wisdom. They have no necessary connection with one another. Knowledge and foolishness, wisdom and ignorance often go hand in hand. A man may be blessed with wonderful knowledge, he may be a marvel to all on account of his learning, depth of insight, and quick apprehension of new truths, and yet he may be less wise than another who cannot even write his own name and is totally ignorant.

There was Seneca, often quoted for his beautiful precepts and lofty morality – a man of great attainments but nevertheless a toady and a miser scorned even by his own corrupt generation. There was Bacon, a man of marvellous erudition and extraordinary intellect, who laid the foundations of modern scientific method and research, and yet was completely unable to discern between right and wrong. There was knowledge enough in ancient Egypt and Chaldaea, Greece and Rome, in Palestine too in the time of Jesus, but wisdom was absent. And so grief, tribulation and ruin came to these lands – as they come to every land where knowledge is exalted but wisdom is wanting. Wisdom is often, like a choice plant in a neglected garden, hampered by weeds which, depriving it of light, air, and nourishment, check its growth. But even in its weakest state, it is far above mere knowledge in its possible development.

Surely the writer of the book of Job knew and tried to teach others the mighty distinction between knowledge and wisdom. He speaks of the abundance of knowledge but asks: 'Where shall wisdom be found? Where is the place of understanding?' Then he proceeds to answer his own question. It cannot be found in the depths of the sea nor in the land of the living. Gold and silver cannot buy it. Precious jewels cannot measure its value. It is hid from the eyes of the living. Only God knows the place thereof. God Himself prepared it, and unto man He said: "Behold, the fear of the Lord, that is wisdom; and to depart from evil is understanding." Wisdom is the chief thing and comes from God alone. It is the understanding between good and evil. The wise man writes: 'Wisdom is the principal thing; therefore get wisdom; and with all thy getting get understanding.'

Undoubtedly the first step towards getting this priceless gift is to be conscious of our need for it. Discerning the difference between good and evil is far more difficult than we imagine. The whole of our character depends on it – and yet we give it so little attention! No doubt there are times when we do try to see what it is right for us to do. But there are hundreds of incidents which have been regulated not by any deliberate, honest decision on our part but only by easy gliding along with the stream of our desire. What we habitually and unconsciously say to ourselves is that we can manage the little concerns of daily life quite easily and that there is no need to get help to decide what is of trifling importance. But things often seem trifling simply because we are not looking at them in the light of right and wrong. There is a right way and a wrong way of doing everything, and we do well to think of that, for in thinking of it a loftier conception of the importance of all life will make itself known to us. We need to have a right judgement in all things. Solomon did not, saying to himself that he was quite equal to the common duties of a king and confining his request for wisdom to great and critical matters of state. The first step away from what is right is often a short one taken thoughtlessly – but it has given a wrong direction to the soul. Many a traveller has been lost because in the darkness and the fog he has turned his face in the wrong direction. Walking along a strange highroad and coming to a parting of the ways we have to stop and think out our position or consult our map. Sometimes walking over the hills we allow our attention to be diverted by the flight or calling of a bird, or by the beauty of the landscape, or by the flowers at our feet, or the dark, lowering clouds which speak of a coming storm; and we find out only when we are off the hardly discernible track that we are following some aimless sleep walk. Constant watching alone keeps us right, and life is a continual parting of the ways. Sometimes we travel by the broad main road – far oftener by the narrow, half obliterated path. The path will lead us astray just as fatally as the broader road, and perhaps more easily.

Never was there more knowledge in our land; never was there greater need for wisdom in all our citizens. 'Knowledge puffeth up.' Do not we see that every day? It is the great sin of our days that we affirm that we can direct our steps. We give no place to God in the ordinary choices and decisions of our daily lives. What do you think of this slogan chalked on the pavement of a Scottish county town last Sunday: 'Remove God from the air and capitalists from the earth.' You shudder, but have we not almost removed God from the world in which we live? There is no safety for you, me, or anyone till we confess to ourselves our need for God. That is Wisdom – to do otherwise is stupendous folly.

Wisdom is none other than the gift of God. Solomon knew that. So did Job. Neither natural ability nor wealth will obtain it for us. The wisest of our fellow men cannot impart it to us. They may point out what is right and help us, but they cannot ever be at our elbow. We must have the power to discern in ourselves. We cannot be like those climbing plants which make a wonderful show when supported by neighbours but fall to the earth when deprived of their support.

We cannot purchase wisdom and our brothers and sisters cannot give it to us – only God can. 'Give thy servant an understanding heart that I may discern between good and bad.' That is a right royal prayer. It goes to the root of all godly living. It is far better to be armed against the hour when the decision has to be made than to cry to God in the midst of the struggle, or to find afterwards that there was no struggle at all but that evil carried all before it. It is one thing to discern between good and bad – another thing to be able to follow the good. No doubt Solomon often asked for strength to hold fast by what was good. But this prayer was not for power but for discernment.

Do not let us mutter that we know well enough what is right and what is wrong. There is no more common excuse than this: 'I did not know it was wrong.' But let us humbly confess that we have lived far too much in wilful ignorance because we have thought that we could find the right way for ourselves if only God would give us strength to walk in it.

What confidence can we have that God will give us wisdom if we ask for it? We have the example of Solomon to encourage us. But we have greater encouragement than that. Is it not one of the great promises of God's Spirit to give all who ask for it this wisdom? Above all His is the Spirit of understanding and wisdom. Our Lord speaks of Him as 'the Spirit of truth who will guide you into all truth'. He is the teacher ever present who can unfailingly tell us right from wrong and who can ever guide us in the commands of Jesus. Till we know right from wrong we cannot do right. Even so we will often do wrong, so strongly towards evil is the bent of our nature. That is all the greater reason why we should strive to get this power of discernment. Until we so strive the Spirit is unable to comfort, guide, or strengthen us.

What we must do is cry for the help of the Spirit that we may discern between good and bad. We need Him now, not tomorrow. Scorn divine aid and, although we may occasionally blunder into what is right, we will but minister to vain glory and self-confidence. Gradually we will more and more neglect God's Spirit till at length we will find it impossible to ask for His aid in the most terrible of perils.

Let us remember that even with the noblest beginnings and the deepest knowledge of our need of God's help we may go far, far astray. Let King Solomon be a warning to us as well as an example. But what will the end be if we never make a start to Godly living – if we just stagger along blinded with our pride? If it is hard to gain the victory with God's Spirit of wisdom dwelling in us, where will we find ourselves if we fight our battles alone?

This sermon was first preached in St Mary's, St Andrews on May 31st, 1903, and later in Holy Trinity, St Andrews in June 1905.

'

The Restoration of Holy Trinity

Mark XIII 1, 2, 31: And as he went out of the temple, one of his disciples saith unto him: "Master, see what manner of stones and what buildings are here!" And Jesus answering said unto him: "Seest thou these great buildings? There shall not be left one stone upon another, that shall not be thrown down. Heaven and earth shall pass away; but my words shall not pass away."

Brothers and sisters, we cannot meet here today for our first ordinary Morning Service without experiencing a great sense of thankfulness. The hand of our God has been good upon us and we have been marvellously helped. The most sanguine of those who worshipped in this place some thirty months ago could not look forward without anxiety. There were many difficulties to be faced – would they all be overcome? There was a call for faith, loyalty and self-denial – would these be forthcoming? However confidence was justified by events, progress was steady, obstacles vanished, and day by day the end came nearer and nearer till at last it was reached. We now enjoy the fruits of our labours by the blessing of God. So it is right that the first word spoken this morning should be an acknowledgement of the goodness of God. He has brought us to this realisation of our hopes; he has guided us through the years of exile and set our feet upon the land of promise. We are still strangers in our renovated church; some little time must pass before we feel quite at home in it.

Many memories cluster round the former building. We see the old seats peopled with familiar faces. There we sought God's pardon and knew His peace. There we found comfort in the great sorrows of life and gave thanks for signal mercies and daily benefits. There were great days in the past, great preachers speaking for the Lord, and joyful days of Communion when God seemed very near. These memories are all very precious. But already there are new memories. Forty, sixty, perhaps even eighty years hence our successors will recall the opening Service and the crowded Table of the Lord last Sunday. The same stones surround us which so many generations have looked upon. The same psalms will be sung; the same Gospel will be preached; the same aspirations will arise in us; the same resolves will be made. All the change has been of external things. We will soon feel again at home and settle down – not to indolence and selfishness but, by the help of God, to work with increased effort for the welfare of all in our parish and in our world. We have reached a summit, but not *the* summit. There are greater heights to scale. God has helped us to the vantage ground we now occupy that we may be able to do greater things still. What we have been enabled to do we must not regard as an end in itself or we will turn our glory into shame. Are we thankful to God? Then let us show our thankfulness in more abundant labours for our fellow men and women. The programme we set ourselves ten years ago has been carried out – the Halls have been built, this Church has been restored, but these things are the preparation of the army for the fight not the battle itself. Who of us may carry on the contest, God knows, but the call to it is clear.

"And as He went out of the temple, one of His disciples saith unto Him: 'Master see what manner of stones and what buildings are here!' And Jesus answering said unto him, 'Seest thou these great buildings? There shall not be left one stone upon another that shall not be thrown down'." Our Lord spoke of the great temple at Jerusalem and He knew that the renowned city with its splendid temple would be destroyed. Perhaps He was minded that, when the fulfilment of His prophecy came, the remembrance of His words might be some sort of consolation as they told of His foreknowledge and His unwavering certainty of the future. The end of that famous building came quickly, its demolition was complete. All that man has made must one day perish; the whole material universe must perish for heaven and earth shall pass away. We look around upon the walls of this place of prayer which was built with so much toil, skill and cost, we dwell with satisfaction upon the strength and beauty with which they are stamped, and we hope that for generations and centuries they will stand here to witness for God in this city, and yet we know that they cannot last for ever. Who can foretell the future history of this church? Will it be guarded by the piety and affection of posterity? Will vigilant eyes detect every sign of decay and tender hands bind up the weak parts? Will pious hearts labour to add beauty as the years roll past? God grant it may be so. But its doom is written – 'heaven and earth shall pass away'. Nature is a great leveller. All around us every valley is being exalted and every mountain is being brought low. Man can retard the process here and there – nowhere can he arrest it. In spite of his utmost care moth and rust bring corruption. The day must come when this work of ours shall pass away – not, please God, till it has served for an age its noble purpose helping many a weary soul and acting as a door to the Kingdom of Heaven to rich and poor, young and old. This is not a building to eternity. That in which we glory as the evidence of man's potency must sooner or later betray his impotence.

But there are things which survive to eternity. One is character. As this church was built so must we seek to build up character. Stone by stone it arose, each block laid in its place by thought and toil. "You cannot dream yourself into a character," said Froude, "you must hammer and forge yourself one." We must build patiently and unwearyingly. We must search after all that is strongest and richest and seek to make all true, not only what is seen but even what is hidden from view. Whatsoever things are true, whatsoever things are lovely, whatsoever things are pure – these are the materials with which we must build. All that we can receive from the best of men, all that we can quarry from the Bible, all that we can learn from Christ, the great Master Builder we must bring to aid us in our work. When we build for eternity we must see that no unworthy thought mars our design and no unworthy work imperils the stability of the building.

Our church teaches another lesson. Sometimes the innocent, upright character of youth becomes tarnished and even ruined. The once fair building becomes disfigured and unsightly. To restore it to beauty and strength may take vastly greater resources and labour than would have been required to preserve it from decay, but it can be done. Character can be restored. Falsehood, weakness, selfishness and ugliness can be expelled and all restored to something better. As you can take the fragments of a ruin and make them a noble fabric, so by the grace of God can beautiful characters be fashioned anew out of the broken fragments of lives. Let the story of our church these last years be a parable to anyone who is conscious of having fallen from purity, truth and love bidding him arise, stand on his feet and be restored. All is not lost so long as God's voice still speaks to us. We cannot undo things that have been done. But we need not idly wring our hands in despair. Let us rise up and build trusting in God that He will help us and we will not labour in vain.

Neither the building of character nor the words of Jesus pass away. What is the purpose of this or any other Christian church? Is it not the proclamation of the words of Jesus and the worshipping of the Father whom he has revealed? What words are like His? Who gives any reply to the greatest questions man can ask except Him? Who else can tell us of our origin and our destiny? Who else can tell us how we are to live and what is to be our fate? The words of Jesus are not like those of many great teachers which serve their day and then are forgotten. Never were men more earnestly seeking to understand and obey these words. Many who do not share our beliefs regarding Him are nevertheless full of insistence on the supreme value of all He said. Never were more men prepared to cry out with Peter: 'Lord, to whom shall we go? Thou hast the words of eternal life.' They have not passed away, they have not lost one atom of their influence because they deal with the deepest needs of the human soul. They carry with them authority, they reach loftiness, they contain depths of wisdom and love which ensure their abiding power in the world. All other words might pass away and we would indeed be the poorer, yet having Christ's we are rich for ever. But if it were possible that men should forget all He has said where would we stand? We would be groping in the darkness, haunted by fears that could not be allayed. The words which for 2,000 years have brought peace to men's hearts and stirred them to great acts of heroism and love will maintain their sway to the end. "Never," said a great preacher, "never in the morning leave your room without asking what do these blessed words … say to me for guidance or support, or instruction, or warning in the work of the day? Never lie down at night without bringing what has been thought and said and done to be judged by the words of the Divine Teacher, that you may ask His pardon where you have gone astray or thank Him for His grace where you have been enabled to conquer. To make those words the rule of life and thought must be the effort of a true Christian."

May God grant that from this pulpit there may ever continue to be set forth with all faithfulness the words spoken by His only-begotten and well-beloved Son Jesus Christ, and that those who hear these words may know from personal experience that they are the words of Eternal Life.

This sermon was preached at the first morning service in the restored Holy Trinity on December 12th, 1909 and, suitably adapted, at the first anniversary of the dedication of St John's, Dundee in September 1915.

Render unto Caesar

Romans XIII 7: Render therefore to all their dues; tribute to whom tribute is due; custom to whom custom; fear to whom fear; honour to whom honour.

These words are a clear echo of those spoken by our Lord in answer to the question about political authority put to Him by the Pharisees. It was a cunning plot which was laid with the object of catching Him out. We have only to remember the ever watchful jealousy of Rome, the reckless tyranny of Pilate, and the low artifices of Herod and those in authority in Jerusalem, to understand that even the slightest error on the part of Jesus would have been fatal. He would have been finished and His enemies would have triumphed. But He had no difficulty in giving a definitive reply. Paul takes up the same position when he writes of the attitude Christians should assume towards established power, whether Christian or heathen.

Obedience, he says, is due in all lawful matters. Of course if the civil power requires us to break the law of God – for instance, if anyone were ordered to offer incense to idols as so many early Christians were ordered to do – then there comes into play a higher law, we must obey God rather than man. Also, if commanded to violate the common laws of humanity then too a higher and more general law than that laid down by the State demands our disobedience to that command. But it would be fatal to all authority and it would be fatal to the State if everyone was allowed to treat the laws as he chose. The teaching of our Lord and His Apostle is perfectly clear on this matter. We can well imagine that the government of Rome was in some ways not only distasteful but even abhorrent. They must have detested its heathenism and loathed its want of heart; but they did not let their feelings drive them into opposition. They set themselves to support the power that existed, not because it was what they would have had it to be, but because it was there and because it was performing duties which were essential for order. Christianity does not observe neutrality between anarchy and government – it throws its whole weight against the former. The people dwelling under the rule of Rome had to pay taxes, for no government can be carried on without expense. Christians must not fail to discharge this duty. They must share in the support of the government under which they certainly reap some benefit. Government moreover cannot be carried out without officers, some of whom may be worthless in character – men and women who by their conduct out of their office, and at times in it as well, degrade their ministry and make it very difficult for others to pay the respect due to the power they represent. Nevertheless Christians must distinguish between the office and the holder of the office, and show the deference which is due to the one even though they despise the other. Deference is due also to those upon whom the State has conferred distinction.

St Paul is not stating all the duties of the citizen in this verse. He is dealing with a particular matter – the relationship between subject and ruler. There are duties which the ruled owe to one another and these are of the utmost importance. He does not touch on these save in the following verse he writes: 'Owe no man anything but love' – love being the only debt which cannot be paid off and which the Christian may owe with honour. 'This debt increases the more, the more it is paid; because the practice of love makes the principle of love deeper and more active.'

We ought not to think only of what the State owes us. There are some in the Church who are chiefly concerned with taking as much from it as they can for themselves. They seek its charity and its influence in their business, and they look to it to promote their temporal interests. The Church is to work for them, not they for the Church. We find the same thing in the State. There are many who look on it as a power which ought to be always exerting itself for their special benefit and which is to be made use of for their own profit, but to which they have no dues to pay. This is an utterly wrong conception for true government must always keep in view the interests not of individuals or classes but of the whole body of people. It is a foolish concept for the inevitable result of the withholding of what they owe to the State must be the weakening of the very power whose gifts they so often invoke. A self seeker in the family weakens its influence and hinders its prosperity; it is the same in the larger field of the commonwealth.

We must have a higher idea of rule than that it exists simply for our own benefit. We must recognise that we have to work for its support and the increase of its authority. We must act as honourably towards it as we do towards an individual citizen. Yet is it not true that some who would never dream of deceiving or defrauding a neighbour, and who are scrupulously honest in business and whose word in ordinary affairs is absolutely reliable do not think it necessary to preserve so high a standard in their dealings with government? The false return to the authorities is not regarded as dishonest or mean. Is it only dishonest to defraud an individual? Is it to be called smart and worthy of praise when a community is robbed? Surely such conduct is in defiance of the exhortation 'tribute to whom tribute is due'.

Taxation is at present an increasingly serious matter for us all. We may have our own views as to the justice of taxation. We may doubt the wisdom of how taxes are spent or we may rail against wanton extravagance, but to say 'this tribute should not be asked of me, I do not approve of all that is done and I intend if possible by any means, however crooked, to get rid of paying it' is unfair to the whole body of the citizens, prejudicial to the State, and disloyal to the ruler. There is no spirit of loyalty where there is fraud upon the revenue. Increase in tribute demanded will no doubt increase efforts to escape payment, and that must be borne in mind by the government. No Christian, no true citizen will lie and be disloyal however severe the tribute. Disloyalty may also be shown in breaking the spirit of the law although the letter is observed.

'Custom to whom custom.' Taxation may be indirect as well as direct. Indirect taxation may at times be irritating but the principle involved is the same. It is unpatriotic, disloyal and unChristian to conceal goods liable to duty. In St Paul's day customs were farmed out to private individuals. It was wrong to defraud them and it is equally wrong to defraud the State. To boast of exploits which lessen the national revenue is deceitful and discreditable. And yet otherwise exemplary citizens think it no shame to do these things. The actual offences may be small but the spirit behind them is the same as if they were great and their smallness is due rather to lack of opportunity than lack of desire. It goes without saying that if officials receive in silence money given them in ignorance, money to which the State is not entitled, equal or greater shame attaches to their action.

Nor is it Christian to withhold reverence from those set over us in authority. It is dishonourable to flout such as be in power in the land, even those in lowly positions. He who lowers the dignity of another by churlish acts only shows how little care he has for the stability of the land and the welfare of the people. To give reverence and honour to whom reverence and honour are due is not servility but the declaration of loyalty to the government and obedience to the teaching of Christ.

The nature of the life we lead is dependent on the view of life we take, whether we are continually asking ourselves: 'What do I owe to others, or what do others owe to me?' If the first question is always in our thoughts then we shall be humble, helpful and profitable citizens. If we prefer to dwell upon the second we shall become promoters of discord and disorder thus retarding progress and hindering all that makes for the best interests of our people.

St Paul addresses himself to our dues to the 'powers that be', but we have debts to all men, even to the humblest, payment of which is often overdue. Right living is helpful living. To live is to develop, to communicate, to strengthen life. The question to ask is not what can I get for myself, but what can I do for my fellows?

And if we have dues to all how can we forget God? How dare we pay no respect to God? Is He alone never to be in our thoughts? Woe to us, to the people, and to the State whatever its form of government when the tribute and the reverence due to God are not rendered! It has been written: 'Whatever is taken from the sovereignty of God is added to the sovereignty of the tyrant.' When the dues we owe to God are not rendered and when His sovereignty is rejected, there is no alternative but the reign of brute force. No kingdom, no republic, no nation will survive ultimately so monstrous a declaration of insensate pride and so defiant a repudiation of the universal Creator and Lawgiver. The existence and recognition of human authority depend on respect for divine authority. 'Render unto all their dues.' That way lie order, peace, and life – all other roads lead to hatred, violence and death.

This sermon was first preached in Holy Trinity, St Andrews on July 2nd, 1910, and again in October 1920.

The Holy City

Revelation XXI 10: He showed me that great city, the holy Jerusalem.

'A city is first the ambition and then the despair of man,' it has been said. To many it is the freedom, the simplicity, the peace, the absence of interruption and distraction, and the greater opportunity to study nature that makes country life attractive to so many. The country lends itself to those who seek rest, health and solitude for meditation. The mountains, the wilderness and the pastures have been the scenes of many wonderful events when God spoke to His servants and they sought His presence – events which would have been unsuited to the streets of the city. Jacob at Luz, Moses and Elijah at Horeb, Jesus in the wilderness, on the Mount of Transfiguration, and in the Garden of Gethsemane have perhaps led to the feeling that what is purest and holiest is not to be found in crowded streets – that the countryside is better for the soul as well as for the body. The Psalmist cried out for the wings of the dove that he might 'wander far off and remain in the wilderness'. But it has also been said: 'It is a joy and a privilege to live in a great city.' The hymn writer Horace Bonar wrote:

'Yet despite your earnest pity
And despite its own smoke and din
I cling to your crowded city
Though I shrink from its woe and sin.

The wonders of life and gladness
All the wonders of hope and fear:
The wonders of death and sadness
All the wonders of time are there.

And the home to which I am hasting
Is not some silent glen;
The place where my hopes are resting
Is the city of holy men.'

The tide of life flows with ever increasing force from the country to the city. And yet, the city is also the despair of man, so great are the problems which cry out for attention. Throughout the world cities harbour in their midst misery and vice untold. How can this be remedied? Theorists tell us how it can be done, but practical men are less confident knowing how deep-seated the problem of evil is and how slowly efforts are made. How often legislative, philanthropic, and religious schemes fail to make real and lasting improvement! No wonder some in perplexity pray for God's help to keep our cities small.

It is startling to see that the ideal abode of God's people is not to be found in flowery meadow, among majestic hills, or alongside the ocean, but in a city, the new Jerusalem. Man's life on earth began in the garden; it ends in the eternal city. The tree of life stands in the midst, but it is surrounded by streets, gates and walls, and the nations walk beside it and the rulers of the earth bring their glory and honour to it. This is a higher concept than that of the lonely pair wandering through banks of flowers and shady woods. Love has prevailed. No longer does man shrink from man or the crowd offend the tender heart. No longer do those who wish to rest or to meditate on great things flee to solitude. There is no need of temple or hermit's cell. Fellowship, mutual cooperation, and devotion to God reign supreme – none live unto themselves but all unto God. There is peace everywhere. This is a higher concept than that of men and women scattered abroad in little groups and communities each with their own interests and prejudices, harbouring their own ambitions and jealousies, and priding themselves on their independence of others.

The great city, the holy Jerusalem is a free fellowship bound together not by force but by love.

That great city is not a glorified Jerusalem but a new Jerusalem, an ideal city. Renan describes Revelation's heavenly Jerusalem as 'clumsy, childish, impossible'. We cannot imagine a city 1,300 miles long and broad and high. Such measurements exceed the wildest flights of imagination. But the form of a cube is used to express solidity, stability, and permanence. Unimaginable vastness and glory, and not definitive size are what the language used should impress upon us. This holy Jerusalem is the perfect city – the dimensions of it are equal.

In the life of this city there is no reference to the things men strive for in our earthly cities to minister to their desire for pleasure and enjoyment. We are told of that tree of life whence the nations that are saved shall pluck the fruit and the leaves full of healing virtue; of the water of life of which all may freely drink; of the light given them by the Lord God. But the full bliss of that great city is beyond human comprehension. Other religions have promised heavenly cities painted in very earthly colours, wherein the righteous enjoy the gratification of physical desires. It is otherwise with the followers of Christ who live, think and hope on a higher plane. St John, as St Paul, knew that 'flesh and blood cannot inherit the Kingdom of God'. The joys and glories of Paradise are of a spiritual order. The Psalmist gives us some idea of the new Jerusalem. The great causes of suffering on earth will be absent.

There will be no more *sea*. From the throne of God and the Lamb there flows the river of pure water ever ministering to life. The river preserves and nourishes but never destroys. On its banks grow lush grasses and succulent herbs upon which the beasts of the field feed as they quench their thirst from its waters. The sea offers nothing to the thirsty – its waters speak of separation and its storms strive to overwhelm. In the holy City there are no divisions and no storms.

There will be no more *night*. 'Infinite day excludes the night.' No sunset calls the beasts of the forest to creep forth, and no sunrise summons men and women to their labour. There is no darkness of error, superstition, or ignorance filling the soul with dread, paralysing doubt, or haunting anxiety. All things are revealed and in perfect knowledge there is perfect light. 'There is no darkness but ignorance.' *(Twelfth Night Act IV Scene 2)*.

There will be no more *pain*. Think what that means! How we would struggle and exhaust every means in our power to reach such a place on earth, both for ourselves and for our dear ones! It would indeed be Heaven. That place does not exist on earth, but in the holy City pain cannot exist.

And there will be no more *death*. The last dread enemy is overcome. His work is finished. No more can he snatch away friend from friend and leave the widow and the orphan to the coldness of a careless world. No more death! How hearts leap at the promise!

These are some of the characteristics of the City seen by St John in his vision. Such is Heaven, the City of God. It is not here and it may never be here, but it is set before us not only as the object of hope but as an object of endeavour. It forbids us rest content with the condition of our earthly cities, and it points us in the directions in which we should labour to transform them. Division, ignorance, suffering, death – these are the great evils in our midst and the enemies we are to meet and fight. By all means let us seek to beautify our streets, embellish our buildings, and provide recreation for our citizens. But the achievement of these things may only throw into deeper shadow the things, the far greater things, that may remain undone. That city comes nearest to the ideal in which there is least division between its peoples, in which the greatest efforts are made to dispel the darkness of ignorance, to relieve poverty, to provide for the sick, to repress all which destroys the peace and happiness of families, in which justice, honesty and righteousness prevail, in which those who themselves live in Christ seek most faithfully to deliver from temptation and the bondage of sin their fellow citizens who are spiritually dead. What avails a city to have a famous history, a beautiful situation, the reputation of being a pleasant dwelling place if there be lack of unity, true knowledge, love, compassion, and commitment to Christianity? How many a city bears a fair face which strangers look upon with pleasure and yet is unlovely at heart – its streets splendid, its hidden alleys squalid; its public buildings magnificent, the dwellings of its poor awful; its sources of amusement manifold and ever increasing; its hospitals and almshouses barely sufficient. There is honour, gratitude, and lasting fame to be won by all who will work in Church or State for these great and noble ends in our city life. It is for all citizens in positions of public trust to make sure that nothing enters our cities that defiles and to labour incessantly to drive out all that should not be found in the heart of a community.

No more division, no more pain, no more ignorance! Let us make the place of our dwelling a little more like the holy Jerusalem. You love your city and it is a great trust in your hands. It is, it will be, what you make it, 'whether by your intelligence, your probity, your purity, your disinterestedness, or by your folly, your carelessness, your dishonesty, your baseness'. In the words of the well known preacher Pearson McAdam Muir of Glasgow Cathedral: 'To be faithful and useful citizens of the imperfect city in which we have our home is no unfitting preparation to be citizens of the perfect city that is to come. It is only as we each and all are subject to the rule of Christ our King; as we fulfil His law in the bearing of one another's burdens; as we cease from selfish absorption in our own affairs and pleasures; as we yield ourselves, directly or indirectly, officially or unofficially, in His spirit, to the service of our brothers, sisters and neighbours – it is only thus that the holy City, the new Jerusalem, which was seen coming out of Heaven, will be found to have been set up and established on earth.'

This sermon was first preached in Holy Trinity, St Andrews on November 13th, 1910 for the 'kirking' of the Town Council, and later in St Mary's, St Andrews in January 1911, in Rutger's Presbyterian Church, New York in October 1913, and again in Holy Trinity in May 1919 when Sir Douglas Haig was in church.

A Christmas Message

Luke II 15: Let us now go even unto Bethlehem.

No town or city is regarded by all Christians with such tenderness and affection as the little town of Bethlehem. It is enshrined in their hearts. Other cities are admired on account of their magnificence, their wealth, their treasures, the place they hold in history, the great events they have witnessed, and the dread power of the rulers who have dwelt in them. Bethlehem has no such claims. Jerusalem itself which to the Psalmist was the 'joy of the earth' is ever darkened by the awful tragedy which was enacted without its walls at Calvary. We think and speak of it in subdued tones – full of great interest it nevertheless conveys the impression of being an accursed city. But Bethlehem brings to us only peace and joy. It speaks only of love and gentleness – rebuking all angry thoughts and subduing hatred. It calls on men to lay aside their arms, to cease from pride, selfishness, and oppression, to unite against evil, to bear one another's burdens, to be humble and meek. We sing of Jerusalem the Golden, resplendent in beauty and matchless in power, but there is no such Jerusalem for those who have not found their way to Bethlehem – the Kingdom of Heaven is prepared for the poor in spirit. From Bethlehem there has gone forth the sweetest, purest, kindliest influence ever known, ever to be known, in our world. The little child born there in weakness and poverty has been leading men and women slowly but surely throughout the centuries to higher conceptions of life and duty, to fuller knowledge of justice, mercy, and charity. The progress is un-doubted – the source of that progress cannot be called in question. There may be the greatest diversity of opinion as to the nature of the child Jesus – there can be no denial of the renewal of the world which began when He was born. The very name Bethlehem calls up in us more charitable thoughts and leads us on to forgive injury and practise benevolence. It moves us to give evidence of love for others. The good wishes and the gifts which pass from lip to lip and hand to hand today – what are they but the manifestation of love which is the greater because we think of the love of God made known at Bethlehem and of the duty of loving one another as He has loved us.

It is good for us to go in thought to Bethlehem this morning and once more have our hearts inclined to charity. For our love is still confined within too narrow bounds. It is still too domestic, too much love of family or class. We love them that love us and it is well, but the teaching of the manger is that we should love all. There are many barriers yet to be surmounted – barriers not insurmountable where love is given its way, because to the cradle in Bethlehem there came the representatives of all classes and all nations.

First came the shepherds whose words we have before us as our text. The story of their coming is, like the story of the Nativity, characterised by extreme simplicity. The Gospels narrate no wonders apart from the words and songs of the angels. Fiction would have surrounded the great event of the birth of the Divine Child with signs and portents – and in fact it has done so. In the apocryphal Gospel of St James there is a vivid description of the pause of awe-struck nature. The heavens were motionless, the birds were still, workmen lay on the earth, 'and everything which was being propelled forward was interrupted in its course'. But it was not so, everything went on as usual. The only interruption was that the shepherds left their flocks and hastened to the little town to see the child, 'the Saviour, Christ the Lord'. To these representatives of the toiling masses of humanity the great announcement came first. From the very beginning the message of Salvation was delivered to the weary and heavy laden. It was not when Jesus found the great and learned turning a deaf ear to

His words that He turned to the poor and uneducated. He sought the latter first of all. The shepherds were directed to Bethlehem because to such as them the birth of Jesus meant vastly more than it did to others holding positions of greater authority and independence. In coming and revealing Himself to them He came to all who toiled on land and sea – as the Artist has so beautifully and powerfully depicted in our great east window, to those who sow and reap, to those who build and spin, to all who supply food and fashion raiment for our bodies, to all who erect and beautify our homes. The few peasants who gazed with reverence on the babe lying in the manger on that winter morning were the first of untold multitudes who have knelt in adoration before the Child of Bethlehem. Is it not true that as the Gospel has spread Christ has been welcomed at first by the masses rather than by those of superior station in life? And if there is without doubt today a loud voice lifted up against Christianity in many parts of Christendom, if there are many of the toilers who speak as if Christ had no message for them, surely it is not that His religion is unsuited to their needs but that they have been given or conceived for themselves a wrong impression of His purpose and power on earth. The very evils of which they complain are those which He came to remove by the constraining influence of love. That love works quietly and gently, but it works continuously for the plant springing from the seed scattered over the cradle's edge by the Infant hand spreads in ever widening circles and thrusts its roots deeper and deeper wherever it falls. The revolt against Christian doctrine springing from irritation through the lack of charity too often displayed by those who profess great faith serves a good purpose, for it draws attention to practical religion and, as it has done before, fills Christ's Church with nobler aims and fuller energy. God uses the revolt for His own purposes before it passes away. Love must prevail – it is the greatest power in the world.

Afterwards others went to Bethlehem. Wise men from the east sought out the Infant Saviour. We may put aside as mere surmise the belief that there were three kings who came with a great retinue of followers. These ideas have been perpetuated by the great painters to whose reverent ability we owe so much even if they have gone further than they can find warrant for in Scripture in their desire to do utmost honour to Jesus Christ. But we learn from the visit of the Magi that Christianity appeals to the intellect as well as to the heart, to those who are able to offer rich gifts to the cause of Christ as well as to the comparatively poor, to the Gentile as well as to the Jew. This too can be seen in that window where we see Art and Science, Astronomy, Philosophy, and Medicine, all that is highest in learning and noblest in life worshipping the Christ. Not first at the manger but yet from the beginning those who do the world's thinking, the brain toilers, are found at the side of Jesus. In after years it was the same – the fishermen disciples were first, then came Joseph of Arimathea and Nicodemus. In Apostolic days Peter was labouring for Christ as Paul was perse-cuting the Church. The intellect responds more slowly than the heart, and yet where it does respond how great its service can be! Let us thank God for the wise and learned who have contended for the Faith, remembering that the great have always been drawn to Bethlehem – content to learn the lessons of humility and love before going forth into the world declaring in word and deed their simple belief in Jesus Christ. There are those who say that Christianity has had its day – that it is falling before the march of intellect and through the divisions and wrangling of sects. Let us have courage for the great and good will always be found on His side who speaks of love. They cannot but be drawn by thoughts which have made Bethlehem so great in the history of the world. Jesus was humbled so low not only for our salvation but for our example. Bethlehem says to all who would be honoured and beloved that they must become as little children. This is the great conversion, which stands at the beginning of the Christian life. Pride of will, intellect, and independence, pride of place and consideration, pride of envied possession – all these things which the wisest strongly condemn are brought low at Bethlehem. It is good that the wise go thither that they may be set free from these obstacles to the highest and most beautiful life.

It is well that today we should have our thoughts brought back to the message of Christmas which bids us be gentle and kind hearted, humble and loving. It is well for us to spend this day in thought at Bethlehem worshipping the Infant Saviour, seeking His help to be simple and single hearted, striving to have in us that mind which was in Him. It is well that in the Holy Sacrament of His Body and Blood we should offer a spiritual oblation of all possible praise to God for His unspeakable gift.

This sermon was first preached in Holy Trinity, St Andrews on Christmas Day 1910, and again on Christmas Day 1921.

Patrick Macdonald Playfair at the time of his appointment as Minister of the
First Charge of Holy Trinity in 1899

St Andrews looking down South Street towards Holy Trinity Church from the St Rule Tower c. 1900.
Note the now demolished Priory in the foreground.

Courtesy of St Andrews University Library Special Collections

Holy Trinity Church from the south – 1767 by John Oliphant.
Courtesy of St Andrews University Library Special Collections

A postcard of the nineteenth century church from the south-west.

The nineteenth century church from the south-east.
Courtesy of St Andrews University Library Special Collections

The nineteenth century church from the north-east.
Courtesy of St Andrews University Library Special Collections

*Interior of the nineteenth century church
as remodelled by Robert Balfour 1798–1800.
Courtesy of St Andrews University Library Special Collections*

*John Knox pulpit,
formerly in Holy
Trinity Church now
in St Salvator's
Chapel.*

*Photograph by
George Washington
Wilson.*

*Courtesy of St
Andrews University
Library Special
Collections*

Items from the nineteenth century church retained in the restored Holy Trinity
Church 1909 – Medieval Choir stall, Bishop's Branks and so-called Cutty-stools.
Courtesy of St Andrews University Library Special Collections

Looking down on the canopied pulpit from one of the galleries
of the nineteenth century church.
Courtesy of St Andrews University Library Special Collections

The Restoration of Holy Trinity under way in 1907.
Courtesy of Holy Trinity Church Collection

The restored Holy Trinity Church in 1909 – Architect's drawing.
Courtesy of St Andrews University Library Special Collections

PRESENTATION

TO THE

Reverend Patrick Macdonald Playfair, D.D.

AND

Mr Charles Stuart Grace, W.S.

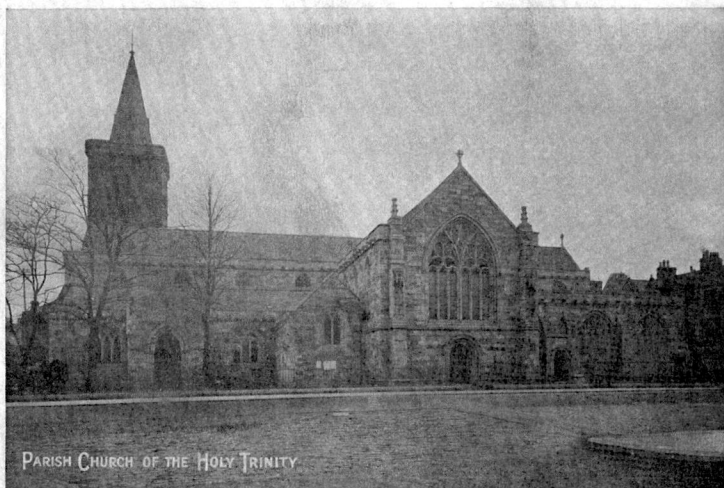

PARISH CHURCH OF THE HOLY TRINITY.

TOWN HALL, ST. ANDREWS,
28TH MARCH, 1911.

Chairman, - - SIR RALPH ANSTRUTHER, Bart.

Presentation ceremony programme.

Dr Patrick Playfair (left) leads the golfer and Elder of the Kirk Old Tom Morris's funeral procession through the Catheral cemetery 1908. His own funeral procession was of comparable length in 1924.

Courtesy of University of St Andrews Library Special Collections

TO THE MEMORY OF TOM MORRIS .
BORN 16 JUNE 1821, DIED 24 MAY 1908 :
AN ELDER FOR 18 YEARS IN THIS PARISH :
COURTEOUS , KINDLY, UPRIGHT , DEVOUT .
GENEROUS IN RIVALRY, MODEST IN VICTORY
HE WAS BELOVED AND HONOURED
BY FRIENDS OF ALL RANKS .

Memorial to Old Tom Morris, famous golfer and Elder of the Kirk for eighteen years who died in 1908

The Miracles of Christ

John XIV 12: He that believeth on me, the works that I do shall he do also; and greater works than these shall he do; because I go unto my Father.

The works of a man are quite as helpful in revealing his nature as are his words. The deeds of many furnish apt illustration of their teaching; the deeds of others only serve to show the falseness of their speech. It is reasonable and fair to try one who claims to be a leader of thought and a teacher of morality by his own life for it is ever true that 'by their fruits ye shall know them'. Deeds may indeed be as eloquent as words.

In the Gospels we have recorded for us the words and works of Jesus which have led to the production of all that is greatest in art, literature, government, philosophy, and philanthropy – all that is best, truest, and most lovely in the achievements of man. For that reason alone we need to give them constant consideration. There is no man who can claim to have exhausted their depth and significance. No generation will ever arise so lofty in aim, so noble in endeavour, and so successful in the pursuit of charity and truth. For our Lord's words are eternal, they do not pass away, 'they are spirit and they are life'. They have been imparting life ever since they were spoken and that power of giving life they possess today without diminution. The Holy Spirit of God has enabled these words spoken so long ago to touch 'the mind, the will, the conscience with the force and freshness of a living voice' when they are still read or heard with prayerful thought.

But it is the same with Christ's works. They too have their message for all time, done in the first place for others but also for us. If He spoke no idle words, He also performed no idle works. Everything is full of instruction lending emphasis to His doctrine and illustrating by a series of sublime pictures the truths which He spoke.

The works of Jesus are of two kinds – ordinary and extraordinary, those which accord with the observed rules of nature and those which overstep the bounds of such observation. All are full of instruction but all are not regarded with equal respect. As some cast aside words attributed to Jesus so some cast aside certain works narrated as performed by Him. The works commonly spoken of as miracles have for long been a battleground. They are for many a stumbling block in the way of accepting Christianity. Yet it would seem impossible to have a Gospel without them. They are so much a part of Christ's teaching that to separate them from it is beyond man's skill. There are those who would put together all the great words of Jesus such as the Sermon on the Mount and leave out whatever some find difficult to believe. However, the broad-minded teaching about the observance of the Sabbath depends on two miracles wrought on that day, and the beautiful address on the Bread of Life is linked with the Feeding of the Five Thousand. Indeed the representation of Christ as the Good Physician and healer of man's body, the source of that great philanthropic movement which has covered Christendom with hospitals owes its rise to the astonishing power He showed over grievous and apparently hopeless diseases. But we must remember that Jesus never said that what He did was contrary to nature – He spoke of His deeds as works or signs. Today we should be chary of saying what is or is not contrary to nature. The discoveries have been so numerous and stupendous of what can be affected within its laws that it is foolish to dogmatise on this subject. Much of what is familiar to us as part of our daily life would not so long ago have been regarded as impossible. Till we know all of nature's law we cannot say what is or is not possible; and man will never know that. There is some controlling force which we believe to be that of a Divine Person. There is a good illustration used long ago by Archbishop Trench: 'When I lift my arm, the law of gravity is not, as far as my arm is concerned, denied or annihilated; it exists as much as ever but is held in suspense by the higher law of my will.' In our experience some works may exceed the laws of nature as we know them, but it does not follow that they exceed the laws of *all* nature.

Too much has been made of miracles as proof of the Divine power of Christ. They were not so much proof of His Revelation as parts of it. They were declarations in deed of God's will regarding men and of the laws which should regulate man's conduct towards God and man. The whole aim and purpose of the miracles of Jesus was for good. Others have claimed to work miracles but such alleged wonders have been devoid of meaning and profit, mere attempts to impress others with a sense of the worker's power. They are not worthy to be put alongside the signs of Jesus which are not merely proofs of His power but also superb revelations of His holy love.

But, an even greater miracle than any He worked is Christ Himself. That He should have lived that pure and spotless life; that He should have brought new courage, hope and joy into the world; that He should have taught a religion which has turned the world upside down; that today He exerts a power incalculably greater than any other person living or dead; that to Him the wisest and best look for the destruction of evil, the redress of all wrong, and the coming of the new heaven and new earth; that He who was born and lived in poverty surrounded by a few loving but humble followers and died a death of shame should have done all this is surely the most wonderful event the world has seen! If we realise what all this means we will be less perplexed by His recorded works.

However we must not place too much stress upon these works for 'greater works than these shall He do'. Following the day of Pentecost the wonder of a soul delivered from sin and death through the Spirit of God brought to him by a single preacher of the Gospel is a greater work than deliverance from bodily disease and even death.

But the miracles of Jesus also have their moral side. The six represented in the window dedicated today are no exception. What do they teach us?

We see the healing of the blind man. Never had he beheld God's beautiful world. Others told him of its wonders; in the morning he heard the singing of the birds; he went out into the fresh air laden with the flowers' sweet scent; he felt the warmth of the noonday sun – but bird and flower and sun he had never seen. How he longed to see! How he hated the blindness! And there standing in the white robe of purity is He who is the enemy of all darkness, who says, 'I am the light of the world', and gives him sight. We who follow Christ must cast away the works of darkness, hate all blindness, and ask power to see aright – striving to know all that is good and true and take the sight Christ can alone give us.

Here is the poor friendless man at Bethesda's pool who for eight and thirty years has been afflicted with helplessness and for long has waited in vain for a chance of healing. Hope must be well nigh dead for there are so many others seeking what he seeks and only one at a time can be cured. But his perseverance is rewarded and the long, weary years come to an end. Jesus puts his earnestness to the proof and rising up he is healed. He who has no other friend has always Christ. Without Him we may spend long years in misery but when He visits us, when we receive Him then new power comes to us and joy fills our heart.

Here are the fishermen who have toiled all night and taken nothing, and with them in the boat is the Master. He bids them let down their nets again, and, tired and dispirited though they be, they obey. Obedience is rewarded. We are to persevere in all things that are good; to listen in the midst of our labour for the Divine voice; to be sure that in obeying the call of duty we will not lose our recompense.

Here again are the Master and His disciples on the renowned lake in their frail craft. The storm which has swept down on them with lurid thunder clouds and terrific lightning flashes threatens them with destruction. They have wakened their sleeping Master and now He rebukes the wind and the waves. Soon all will be calm again. 'Our life is like a troubled sea.' Darkness covers us and we are dismayed by the tempest. Courage! He that keepeth thee doth not slumber! He is not unmindful of His own. We cast ourselves upon Him and He restores our peace – for 'the winds and the seas obey Him'.

Here are 5,000 hungry and weary souls and the Saviour is giving them bread. We learn of the love He bears us day by day – not only when sickness or sore distress comes to us. It is He who by the sunshine and the shower, by the seedtime and the harvest, gives food for the use of man; it is in His hands that the bread grows. This is what He taught us to ask for – our daily bread.

And here is Lazarus called forth from the tomb to new life – the Teacher delivers His friend from the power of death. So does He deliver all who love Him. In this world He raises them from spiritual death and afterwards comes the resurrection of the body. Christ is our life. He gives us the victory over death. We must remember that we need Him to give us this new and eternal life.

This is a part of what we may learn from these beautiful scenes. They call us to follow Christ that we may have peace and strength, courage and life. They bid us be charitable and kind to all. They invite us to help the helpless and feed the hungry. They tell us that in obedience to Christ there is perfect freedom and great reward.

God grant that we may receive these lessons and learn from them! God grant that many generations dwelling in this place may have their faith increased, their love quickened, their souls restored as they look on this noble work of Christian art.

This sermon was preached on January 8th, 1911 when the Grace memorial window by Douglas Strachan was dedicated. See illustration 'Six Miracles of Christ'.

Faith and Doubt

Matthew XXVIII 17: When they saw him they worshipped him: but some doubted.

There is no merit in doubt. It is not to be praised – sometimes it may even be hypocrisy. Neither is it always to be blamed, being misfortune more than fault. It is a far from uncommon condition of mind in which however no honest man is content to remain if he can find deliverance. The man who helps his generation and reaps success is not he who forms half-hearted plans and fritters away his power in ever-changing efforts, but that other who is sure of his aims, his position, and his resources. We may not agree with his views, but we admire him who knows what he wants and believes in his cause: that man will always find some to come under the spell of his assurance. We cannot applaud or follow one who has no confidence in himself, or in any other person, or in anything at all. It is not only themselves that such men injure but others as well. There are always some near the boundary line betwixt faith and unfaith who can be swayed with ease one way or the other. Those who doubted that day would have some effect on the others who worshipped Jesus – not on all, but almost certainly on a few whose faith would be weakened, whose joy would be lessened by their cheerless presence, whose love would be cooled by their chilling silence.

'But some doubted.' So it is always. There are some who enter heart and soul into high plans, and some who hold aloof; some who throw themselves eagerly into an undertaking, and some who only throw cold water upon it. Never yet was there a great teacher whom men revered but some doubted. Never yet was there a great discovery acclaimed by men but some doubted. Never yet was there a great scheme, a great task, a great reform, a great campaign entered upon but some doubted. Never yet was there a great movement for the welfare of mankind but its promoters had, if not to face opposition, at least to resist the down-dragging weight of the doubters. The work, heavy enough in itself, was made more onerous still by those who sought out with assiduous ingenuity every unpleasant possibility, pointed to and published every conceivable danger, magnified every difficulty and obstacle. True, they could not make the enterprise any more hazardous by all their prognostications of evil, or the burden one ounce the heavier; but often have they rendered the heart of the toiler less buoyant and increased faith's struggle for supremacy. All the great achievements of History have been brought about by men and women who had faith; and in spite of all attempts made to sap its very foundations. Every great victory has been gained by faith although doubt strove to paralyse the sword arm. The story of Christ's Church is the story of faith's triumph over doubt within her fold as well as over foes outside. Her experience has been like that of Nehemiah when he was rebuilding Jerusalem, who had not only to guide the workers on the walls and prepare to meet Sanballat in battle, but had to overcome the timidity and faintheartedness of some of his own people, who began to cry out that he had undertaken too great a task, that their strength was failing and well-nigh spent. Every great work done for Christ, every effort for the conversion of the world to Him, every mighty movement towards freedom and purity and unity has been taken by those who worshipped Him, in spite of the protestations of opponents and the fears of the doubters.

Doubt is a canker eating at the heart, a poison stealing o'er the brain, a vampire sucking the red blood of life; but faith is the magic potion stealing the nerves of men, making the will indomitable and the whole form glow with fire and force.

Some doubt, but be it ours to worship – to set stout heart and hand to all which will promote the cause of Christ and truth, to 'hew down wrong' and build up that which makes for righteousness and God. We see Him not who showed Himself to men on earth in mortal form, yet sure enough we hear His voice urging us on to actions worthy of the cause we own. They worshipped Him of old who met Him at the tryst, so let us worship Him who speaks to us, and strive to do His will. It is not for us to heed the cries and obstacles they raise whose hearts are cold and faint. With prudence let us work but never pause through fear of taunt, or ridicule, or greatness of the task. Let us have faith in God, and man, and self. What we can do we know not till we try. We must go onward and must strain upward who are slaves of Christ, counting no cost too great, no toil too hard if we may do His work. They tell us our great quest may fail, that we try something past our powers to do, that time and nature are against us. Yet we must heed them not. We work not for ourselves alone but for generations yet to come – for God, for Christ, for man, for ages without end as well as time.

And what if they be right who doubt and they who worship wrong? What if our hopes for victory of Christ be vain? What if the schemes we cherish languish unfulfilled? What if we toil and strive and strain yet compass not the grand result? What if Cassandra's prophecies of ill come true, and lies not truth prevail, and wrong not right, and every noble purpose come to nought? What if Christ's Church be doomed, Christ's life a fable proved, Christ's brethren's trust be unavailing found? What if the dark, cold grave be the end of all, and those we lose be gone from us for ever, and good men have an equal end with bad? Even then is it not better far to journey on through life with certain mind, with steadfast heart and even step, than stagger through the endless fog of doubt, or fear to move lest we should go astray? Is it not better far if our whole life be only this – full of hope and strength and peace? Is not one week of glowing sun and radiant life worth more than seven sad, sombre weeks of gloom? Is it not better that our week of life be filled by noble impulse, high enterprise and eager work than given up to supine idleness and hopeless apathy? Is it not better to soar heavenwards and carol in the morning sun and carry gladness to the heart weary of watching through long hours of night and to the man who goes forth to his labour day by day – than to be caged and dumb? If this brief life be all then let it be a life of strength and confidence and peace, not weak and torn with haunting fears and harassed with conflicting thoughts. Let it be full of loving help to others and devoid of grave offence to even the weakest one around. Let us by bright example lead on men and women to glad and useful lives.

It is better to have high ideals though we may not reach them, to attempt great things though we may not ourselves see them accomplished than to live sordid, shrinking, selfish lives. Our ideal may commend itself to them with some greater power. Our plan others may make their own and carry out, so the high aim at last becomes fulfilled, and what we laboured for is man's at length. Be it ours to worship. Be it ours to bow down to all that speaks for justice, tenderness and love – to worship Christ 'o'er the tumult of our life's wild restless sea', who calls us to Him, that He may give us work to do, and in the doing of it rest, to follow Him, sacrificing self to the fine promptings of our inmost heart, to do all in His will that we may know the truth. Let us think nought too hard which makes us more like Him and nought too costly which may do Him reverence and bring Him praise. Let it be ours to worship Him, then will we know of His power to help and the sure satisfaction of our hopes to come. We will prove by virtue of our lives that Christianity is no sweet dream from which we dread to wake, but that blest faith which rouses us from sloth and sin, conquers doubt and death, prompts us for the dear Lord's sake to venture on high paths of enterprise, and guides us through the tomb to Heaven itself. 'He that overcometh shall not be hurt of the second death.'

This sermon was first preached at Crathie before King George V and Queen Mary on September 29th, 1912, and later in Rutger's Presbyterian Church, New York in November 1913, and at St Andrews in Holy Trinity in August 1915 and in St Mary's in September 1915.

Outbreak of World War I

Numbers XXXII 6: Shall your brethren go to war, and shall ye sit here?

At last the storm which had been brewing so long has burst upon us. The war predicted by many and which wise men warned was at hand has broken out – a war which has no equal in history either in the number of nations involved, or in the size of the armies engaged, or in the magnitude of the interests at stake, and which may not end in a patched up peace but must be carried out till utter defeat and bitter humiliation have been endured by one side or the other. The wolf has thrown off the sheepskin disguise and revealed himself as he is – treacherous, merciless, savage. The nation from whom we have been told to borrow our philosophy, our theology, and even our Christianity has shown itself to be animated by a medieval spirit of ferocity; its soldiers by repute guilty of actions unacceptable here but which are applauded by their Emperor. We stand today amidst greater perils than have ever before faced our nation. The enemy means to annihilate us and our allies if he can. Let us make no mistake. This is not a case of a little discomfort, a considerable expense, and a certain curtailment of Empire till the tables be turned – it is a case for us of life and death.

Our nation, which has been content to pay for a small army and which has gladly accepted that our manhood should not in times of peace be prepared for possible war, has been forced into a quarrel, which it neither originated nor desired, with two nations in which every able bodied man is a trained soldier. We have taken the part of the underdog – not for the first time in our history – and by the blessing of God we hope to overthrow, along with our allies, the power of the oppressor.

In this country we are slow to awake at such a crisis. We rely on the bravery of our little army, and comfort ourselves with the reflection that as in the past all will work out right in the end. We do not yet realise the strength of the foe, the danger of invasion, and the horrors which inevitably accompany the presence of a hostile army in our land. But at last there are signs that our people are awaking from indifference and insensibility.

Much is being done to help with the conduct of the war but the clamant need is for more to be done. Five weeks have passed and only half of the 500,000 men requested by Lord Kitchener have been enrolled. More are needed and needed at once. Months must pass by before the recruit of today is fit for active service. There is no time to be lost. We have come to our senses late, yet not too late to avert disaster, if the nation is now in earnest. Our Presbytery has asked all its members to take every opportunity 'to exhort the young manhood in their respective neighbourhoods to stand up in response to their country's call'. The injunction was hardly necessary for we are well aware of the danger facing us. Every true Briton, man and woman, must help, and with speed, to procure recruits for the army. By words of encouragement, by assuming responsibility for wives, children, and dependants, and by, if necessary, showing contempt for the shirker we, who ourselves cannot go on active service, must seek to bring others to fill the ranks. We must act quickly. There are still some to whom we put the question: 'Shall your brethren go to war and shall ye sit here?'

Thank God we have an army that is small in numbers yet maintains the splendid traditions of our forefathers. In the past weeks our soldiers have so borne themselves that the world is ringing with the story of their mighty feats of valour. All honour to those who have been training for the defence of our shores and of whom so many have now volunteered for foreign service, and all honour to those who in the last few weeks have left work, home, and friends at their country's call.

But what of the able-bodied who with ties no stronger than those of their brethren are content to follow the course of inglorious ease? Others have gone to war leaving mother, wife, and children. Why do they sit here? A week ago Lord Roberts addressed a newly formed battalion in London with the following words: 'How very different is your action to that of men who can still go on with their cricket and football, as if the very existence of the country were not at stake. This is not the time to play games wholesome as they are in the days of peace.' Is it craven fear? There is no place for the coward in the King's Army. But what will the craven have to say when peace comes? What will be his share of the blame if there should be defeat? What part can he have in the rejoicings of victory? What will he have to say to his brethren who went to the war while he sat at home? But cravens are not rife amongst us. Apathy is a more deadly evil. 'It is all right, somebody else will go'. How often the excuse is made! You men of Scotland rouse yourselves and arouse others. If you cannot go yourselves then make it possible for another to go. "I cannot go myself, I am too old for active service," said one to me the other day, "but I will take the work of another to set him free." You women too can do much if you possess the old British spirit.

'Mother, stay not thou thy boy,
He must learn the battle's joy;
Sister, bring the sword and spear,
Give thy brother words of cheer;
Maiden, bid thy lover part,
Britain calls the strong in heart.'

Ministers are sometimes criticised for exhorting men to enlist without being expected to act themselves. However, no fewer than eighty

Ministers of our Church, including two members of this Presbytery, have volunteered as Chaplains – a post far from safe. Another neighbouring minister, William Monteith, who a few years ago assisted in carrying on the work of this parish has enlisted as a trooper in the Fife and Forfar Yeomanry – a splendid and brave example to young men in our district. A Divinity student who often read the Lessons here last winter has also enlisted. We hear that recruits come forward in ever larger numbers, but many more are needed. There is no excuse for any who are of proper age and physically fit to sit here while their brethren go to war.

But of course there are many who cannot go to war. All work cannot cease. Many lack strength of body or are too old, but they can surely help. They can inspire others with hope and confidence. They can avoid the spreading of false reports and foolish rumours. They can avoid the language and demeanour of panic. They can support the various Funds which have been opened to relieve the sufferings caused by this war. The women can give and are giving their time and skill in the making of garments for our soldiers and sailors, which will be the more necessary as winter approaches.

We ought also at this time to give to an extent commensurate with our resources. Of course no one can be certain that his or her income will be maintained, but let our giving to these Funds be in proportion to our expenditure in other directions. The National Relief Fund instituted by the Prince of Wales now amounts to some £2,250,000. We applaud such generosity, but in fact it seems miserably small when we consider the enormous amount of suffering which has to be relieved – suffering endured indirectly as well as directly through the war, suffering incurred by others for us. We should bear in mind the national expenditure on amusements and luxuries. The annual expenditure of our people on tobacco is some £24,000,000. The expenditure on drink is about £160,000,000 – that is to say the nation has given to this Fund a sum equal to its drink bill for five days, which does not appear to be extravagantly generous. Make no mistake – a vast number of contributions have been given with no small measure of sacrifice; but it is plain that giving has been niggardly and perhaps by the majority there has been no giving at all. There is a good deal to be ashamed of in the paucity of giving to these Funds. Think what our soldiers and sailors are doing for us and then judge of the adequacy of our offerings for the wounded, the bereaved, and the dependants of our brave men. Would it have been excessive liberality if the National Fund had now equalled half the money spent on the luxury of smoking – if it had been £12,000,000 instead of £2,250,000, or if it had given what it spends on drink in a month?

There is another way in which those who must stay at home can help – prayer. Such a time as this tests our faith in God and our belief in His power to hear and help us. If there be any power in prayer now is the time to make proof of it. Never did our nation need God's help more. If you believe in prayer come and take part in our daily intercession here instead of wandering about the streets or links. Come as a duty; come as a privilege. Come in the spirit of prayer. But do not come merely if it is convenient and you have nothing else to do. Come and you will find help for yourselves at the same time as you implore God's help for others.

There is one more thing to say. This is a time for straight talking. I appeal to you to do nothing to hinder soldiers in the execution of their duty. When here they are not on holiday either for their own or for your amusement. In the past in time of peace when members of the services have been here some of our population have behaved discreditably. Behaviour which was discreditable then would be shameful now. There are men who like to be seen in company with those who are of a different breed and who try to gratify their desire by most improper means. There are young women, whose conduct has been such that all our respectable citizens have been ashamed of them. This is no time for carousing and frivolity. I appeal to all to denounce and prevent by every possible means, forcibly if necessary, all attempts to turn the very terrible times in which we live into an occasion for buffoonery, ribaldry and licentiousness. Let us not gloss over such offences; let us not tolerate the offenders. Let the whole weight of public opinion be brought to bear upon them to compel them to propriety of conduct. Let them be forever accursed who fail in their duty when their country requires the very best everyone can give.

This sermon was preached in Holy Trinity, St Andrews on September 6th, 1914 on the outbreak of World War I.

The Feeding of the 5,000

John VI 12: Gather up the fragments that remain, that nothing be lost.

There is more than one lesson to be gathered from this miracle of the feeding of the 5,000. We wonder at the multiplication of the scant store of food till all were satisfied and at the quantity of fragments which were gathered at the close. The giver of the feast had provided for all with the utmost liberality. There was abundance and even superabundance. Let us note this splendid bounty – like the bounty we experience at God's hand day by day. All around us are lavish gifts far exceeding what is needful. There are so many things which appeal to us through our senses and fill our hearts with gladness. Food for the body is only a small part of the provision made for us. How much there is left over after our needs are supplied! It is the way our Father in Heaven treats us – His is no niggard hand but bountiful to the point of prodigality. There is always more left over.

But there is another reason for our wonder that so many fragments remained after all had eaten. Twelve baskets full of broken pieces of barley bread indicate a certain greed and carelessness on the part of the guests. This meal provided without any effort of their own was not valued as it might have been. This is often the case. What costs us nothing is thoughtlessly used and lightly abandoned. The feasters could not use all that they took and they showed no inclination to consider others who might be in want. There is a rebuke in the order issued by our Lord that 'nothing be lost'! For the Lord of nature, like nature herself, is most bountiful and like nature He works with the 'nicest and truest economy'. There is no waste in nature; everything has its appointed use and is used up. Jesus could not see without disapproval the fragments of wholesome food which lay strewn on the ground whereon the multitude sat. These remains, even though they filled twelve baskets, were a small thing to Him. He had just provided a vastly greater quantity of bread and His power was not exhausted nor even lessened. He could do the same again and again. But in another way they counted for much as they pointed to a habitual disregard of economy. He must not lay Himself open to the charge that He saw nothing to reprove in waste or that there was no call to husband the food because it had been got without effort.

Here we find the rebuke of a very common practice. Because something has become ours without effort we hold it in light esteem. One man has been born in a position of comfort and wealth – does he value his advantages as does another who has only procured them after long years of self-discipline and struggle? Will he not use them with far less care and part with them with far less thought? We see this constantly. The son so often fritters away what the father won with great pains. We find the same in nations. We have come into a great inheritance for which our forefathers suffered as they built it up. How careless we have been! We have lost opportunities and squandered our advantages. We have thrown away as fragments what cost us not one single drop of blood though our ancestors laid down their lives for them. We would have acted otherwise if we had been called upon to pay the price. We have eaten till filled and thought little of those who come after us. We took the centre and threw away the crust. There is one lesson for us today which we must learn. We must realise that we have erred in want of thought, in failure to recognise responsibility, and in forgetfulness of the needs of others. Our generation has been overcome by selfishness; it has been enough that we have been well provided and cared for.

But our Lord did not only rebuke the apparent thoughtlessness of the 5,000, He rebuked all waste and lack of economy. We should be deeply impressed to see Him demanding what the people had thrown away to be gathered together and preserved. We need to be on our guard against extravagance and against striving after what is unnecessary as well as against throwing away what can and should be made use of. We should practise economy. In the first place we should use the powers of body and mind given to us with economy. That means we should labour after things which will increase usefulness and not throw away our gifts in worthless quests. For we are all gifted in some measure. Our aim must be right and we must pursue it in a right way, neither with too little resolution, nor with undue demand upon our powers. Economy lies between slackness and excess, between partial and extreme use of our strength and faculties. How many lives have been failures or cut short because of error in the one direction or the other? How many vessels might be filled with the waste of our lives! How many baskets might be heaped with wasted possibilities and opportunities! We must strive to use diligently and faithfully all our powers of thought and action. Not one fragment should be thrown away or left unused of all that God has given to us.

Again, we must use aright our material possessions, the things which are not essential. We should be economical. Some may sneer at economy as an old fashioned and out of date virtue. Yet it is the presence or absence of economy which enables us to live honestly and peacefully or leads us to dishonour and adversity. The economical man adjusts his expenditure to his income, gets the most out of everything and avoids extravagance in all directions. He dresses temperately, eats and drinks in moderation, and rations his desire for amusement. He is neither miserly nor reckless in expenditure upon himself. His house is well ordered, his affairs are well managed, and there is no waste in anything with which he is concerned. It is he who is able to help succour benevolent works and befriend others who have fallen on evil days. It is he who stands resolute when trouble falls upon his community. On the other hand he to whom this virtue is strange is apt to be in constant difficulty. Waste is a form of selfishness which leads on to other forms of the same evil. It tends to make a man's thoughts centre on himself when he should be preparing to help others by taking no more for himself than he is able to use profitably and so leaving more for them.

May I impress upon you the urgent need for practising at present the strictest economy? They are foolish who talk lightly of a few weeks more of war, who say, 'It will be over by Christmas'. Even if the German army should be driven out of France and Belgium much would remain to be done. The fortifications of Germany are immensely strong, her army even after losses of appalling magnitude will still be vast in numbers. No one doubts the determination of the Emperor, the ability of his staff and the resolution of his soldiers. It may be that if the German power is overcome its overthrow will be accomplished not so much by the direct assaults of the Allies as by distress following lack of employment, meagre harvests and consequent shortage of food. It is clear then that we must be prepared for a long war. Our industries will suffer and incomes will shrink. Economy, which is always right, is specially called for. Resources must be carefully husbanded and only necessary expenditure incurred. Any excess in food, in dress, in amusement, in any direction is to be strongly condemned and whoever is guilty of it is disloyal and a source of danger to the nation. What at ordinary times calls for mild censure is now culpable extravagance and inexcusable waste. What may then be done or used with innocent satisfaction should now be cause of shame. This is a time when true loyalty calls for the strictest possible care and for obedience to our laws and to the counsels of the wise. We know nothing of the horrors of war as they have been revealed to the inhabitants of Belgium and North-eastern France. Little is asked of us when we are required to be moderate in our desires and their fulfilment. We should practise economy not only to make our own position more secure, but that we may be able to give more for the relief of those who are suffering through the ravages of war. The effort now being made will have to be renewed again and again. Our soldiers and their allies on the field of battle are doing their duty nobly. Then let us do our share in upholding our just cause by well ordered living and generous giving even to the point of sacrifice.

This sermon was preached in St Mary's, St Andrews on September 13th, 1914 and in Holy Trinity, St Andrews on September 20th, 1914, and in Glasgow Cathedral in October 1914 soon after the beginning of World War I.

World War I Easter Sermon

John XI 23: Thy brother shall rise again.

Never since Jesus Christ spoke these words have so many been listening for them and to them. Not only in the peaceful churchyards of the homeland but away in sunny France, in the burning plains of Africa, amidst the snow covered ranges of Caucasus, in the sands of Arabia, in the swamps of the Tigris, on the steppes of Russia, in the pleasure grounds of the Tyrol, beneath the blue waters of the Mediterranean and the grey North Sea, and the Atlantic and Pacific Oceans the thousands of dead have found their resting place during these months of savage strife. Their graves are marked, when marked at all, in simplest, humblest manner. No loving words can lay upon them on this Easter morning the flowers which tell of an affection which death cannot efface. Over them roll the sullen waves and the roar of the murdering guns. Over them rise the shouts of those who strive for mastery, and over them rush the mighty warships of the air and sea drowning the sweet, spring carolling of birds and lading the gentle breeze with poison fumes. Many a thousand hearts are torn today with anguish as they mourn the distant dead. Their sorrow is increased because they cannot stand beside the spot where lies the brother, husband, son, the soul's delight, the faithful friend. To die away from home, to die in battle, or perchance within the hospital ward, to die in the cold, heaving water crying in vain for help – how sad and harrowing an end! But these words break the silence and dispel the gloom – 'Thy brother shall rise again'. The precious life was given again to the sisters of Bethany and joy assumed the place of grief. For what He said would be, He brought to pass.

Furthermore He who spoke to Martha speaks to us. 'Thy brother shall rise again.' But He has given us more than words. For He Himself rose from the tomb wherein His body had been laid by careful, loving hands. He was raised by God and therefore did He raise Himself, for He was God. It has been said: 'We all know what life and power a man's own spirit will often give him. We have heard of spirited men in great danger, or spirited soldiers in battle when faint or wounded who struggle and fight on, doing the most desperate deeds to the last, from the strength and courage of their spirits conquering pain and weakness and keeping off for a time death itself.' Some may have read this tale from the battle front, which we would do well to ponder. When, last winter, the enemy poured into a trench, and almost all the defenders were killed, a French sergeant, grievously wounded, grasped a rifle and began to shoot, crying out to his semi-conscious comrades: 'Stand up, ye dead.' At the wild cry the wounded arose, and the half dead began to shoot with unsteady hands. By a resurrection from the dead the trench was saved.

We all know how men seized by a fit have for a time the strength of ten. 'If then a man's spirit when it is powerful can give his body such life and force, what must it have been with Christ who was filled full of the Spirit? The Lord could not help rising. It was impossible that death could hold Him.' So wrote Charles Kingsley. 'On the third day He rose again from the dead.' 'Thy brother shall rise again.' It is a clear promise and we have an assurance of resurrection in the resurrection of Jesus. 'He that believeth in Me though he were dead yet shall he live; and whosoever liveth and believeth in Me shall never die.'

This assurance which is given us by the Risen Lord is the one thing which can strengthen our hearts today. We may be able to stand at the graveside as Jesus stood by that of Lazarus and wept, or we may not. Our friend may sleep under the green sward with flowers crowding round his head and over his heart or he may lie far beyond seas and mountains where no foot of friend will ever wander, no heart of love will know to search. It makes no difference. The words the Master spoke are not for one age or one race but for all who follow Him in courage, patience, meekness, truth, purity, and love, whatever be their end, wherever they may die.

We sorrow today for the young, the strong, the brave, the chivalrous, the true who have made the great sacrifice and are in our midst no more; but we sorrow not as those who have no hope. There is the great comfort of the Christian faith. We think of them with gratitude and with admiration, of what they gave their country and of the service they rendered us – how they went forth knowing full well the perils they must face, how they loved not the life of hardship, and had no looking for the fight and the killing of fellow men, yet dared and strove because duty called. We do not think of them as those who have lived and died in vain. Wherever they may have fallen they did their share and helped the righteous cause. Death cannot hold them. Truly this is the greatest of days that bids us hope that the dead will rise again. If Christ be not risen then 'earth is darkness at the core, and dust and ashes all that is'. But, courage, 'Thy brother shall rise again'.

Yet it is not only those dear to ourselves or those who have fallen in this cruel war of whom we think this morning. One of the world's greatest men passed away three hundred years ago today. No writer save those who wrote in Holy Scriptures surpasses William Shakespeare in knowledge of mankind, in wisdom, and in dramatic force. His name is a household word in every land. His works are known wherever men speak the English tongue. His words form part of our common speech. If he had never lived how vastly poorer would have been our nation and our race! And yet how miserably we have failed to reap the benefit of his great work! He is a powerful moral teacher with whom the young should be familiarised – yet how small a part is given him to play in the education of our rising generations! Is he wrong who writes of 'the appalling misconception' of the leaders of British education 'about what makes the best teaching for the heart and mind of the young boy and girl of this realm, fitting them to take their places in the Empire and maintain its material and its moral greatness? Precious time is wasted in useless teachings, and not a moment can be spared for this'. But we cannot wonder that they find no room for Shakespeare in the school whose timetable may not take the Bible in. He is without doubt the prince of play writers and yet in this time of bitter distress and suffering it is not Shakespeare's plays which crowd our theatres, but pieces utterly devoid of any moral teaching and entertainments inartistic and imbecile.

It is not amiss to recall here and now his love of country and devotion to its welfare. He was a patriot without doubt. You will find in him no praise of those who love all countries but their own. The coward is not petted but shown up. No one can know him well and not love honourable things – such things as truth and valour, kindness and sacrifice.

'Oh that we now had here but one ten thousand of those men in England that do our work today!' 'After God, Shakespeare created most.' It was, however, not a Briton but a Frenchman who wrote those words.

This sermon was preached on Easter Day, April 23rd, 1916 in Holy Trinity, St Andrews.

The Joy of the Countryside

Song of Solomon VII 11: Come, my beloved, let us go forth into the field: let us lodge in the villages.

The writers of the Bible differ widely in their appreciation of nature. St Paul in his letters hardly mentions anything he saw in lands through which he travelled and which are now famed for the beauty of their scenery and the richness of vegetation. He mentions wheat, olives and vines, but only to illustrate his argument. The glory of a summer day and the loveliness of the Isles of Greece and Bays of Italy seemed to make no appeal to his senses, like St Bernard, who spent a day walking beside the Lake of Geneva without noticing where it was. The same absence of appreciation of nature is found in the letters of the other New Testament authors. Of course the minds of such men were on higher things – they were too intent on the preaching of the Gospel to have time for such ordinary matters. How differently their Master regarded nature. Never was there a mind so oppressed with sorrow for man's sin, so wholly given up to the doing of God's will, so filled with unceasing effort for the good of mankind, and so interwoven with meditation and prayer. And yet never did one live who so keenly felt the beauty, glory and perfection of all around him, and whose words show so clearly that he not only observed but loved with His whole heart every green sward or golden field, every stretch of flower decked meadow, every flock of sheep and lambs, every flight of birds. 'Through Nature He looked up to Nature's God.'

Perfect holiness requires the love of all God's works. Let us not think that those who give themselves up to meditation on things unseen are living on a higher plane than those who in the midst of their daily work find pleasure, recreation and help in observing the marvels of Creation. It may be so, but all who know their Gospel know that it need not be so. The Perfect Life shows that he lacks something who pays no heed to the lilies of the field and the birds of the air.

If in the Gospels we find an ardent love of Nature, so in the Song of Solomon, which sets before us an exquisite example of the love of woman – 'the most tender and inimitable poem that has come down to us of impassioned expression and graceful love' – we find more than anywhere else in the Old Testament, more even than in the Psalms, an intimate acquaintance and deep sympathy with the world in which we live. The poet did not pass along his daily way in life with closed eyes. He was not content with borrowed knowledge to enrich his song, but was evidently a keen observer of his surrounds. His heart leaps for joy amidst the charms of the countryside. The city to give security for the night, but the field and garden to give life and gladness for the day. 'Let us leave the narrow, crowded, steaming streets, my beloved, the day breaks and the shadows flee away, let us go forth into the field, let us lodge in the villages, let us get up early to the vineyards, let us see whether the vine hath budded and its blossom be open and the pomegranate be in flower.'

We find ourselves in an extensive subtropical garden as we read the poem. While the flocks rest at noon we walk with the shepherd lover among the vines and fig trees clothed in the soft green of early summer, and through the shimmering air we look on forests of cedar and cypress, on stately palms and blossom covered fruit trees. Streams of water from Lebanon's snows murmur at our feet and cool the gentle breeze. Our eyes wander over roses, lilies and saffron. The soft cooing of doves hidden from the heart in leafy groves or cloven rocks greet our ears. The young deer shrink through the mysterious woods, the little foxes steal from cover to cover. Myrrh and frankincense, cinnamon and spikenard throw their fragrance all around. Here lie deep peace and complete satisfaction. There is nothing so rapturous in Scripture. This poet loves intensely all that he writes about.

It is good for us to have our thoughts directed thus. The fertile field and the sunny village bring deep content. Here the offspring of the city, doubt, suspicion, irritability, are out of place. Here thought is directed towards faith, confidence and tranquillity. Here is moral no less than physical gain. Wise are the efforts to give our city folk parks for recreation and gardens for use. Wise are they who in the summer flock from town to countryside seeking peace and health. But few who use the city parks know their full good, and few who go to the countryside reap the full benefit of rest and joy which lie to hand. How many find what they deem joy only in more excitement and incessant change! The restlessness of modern life has shorn us of the calm and simple gladness of less strenuous times. The cry is now 'the city', for the city promises amusements of a kind. Yet the study of nature surely leads to the highest pleasure and is available to us all. Few greater blessings can the young receive than the cultivation of a love of nature. To train a child to use his eyes to see the beauty and wonder of all around him, and to be familiar with and to dwell among the members of the lower forms of created life as well known friends is to provide a great resource for hours of leisure and to throw wide open a vast treasure house wherein to wander all through life, ever learning and ever finding new and purest joys.

Here too we shall all acquire knowledge of God, for He who made and who preserves all this cannot be what some say of Him. 'Ye men of austerity and gloom,' wrote Charles Dickens, 'who paint the face of Infinite Benevolence with an eternal frown, read in the Everlasting Book, wide open to your eyes, that lesson it would teach. Its pictures are not wrought in black and sombre hues, but bright and glowing tints; its music, save when ye drown it, not in sighs and groans, but songs and cheerful sounds.'

'Come … let us go forth into the field; let us lodge in the villages.' Amidst the works of God we learn and rejoice and rest as we can never do amidst the works of mankind. There we will know the presence of God. There will our faith in One who never fails in power and never wanes in love be strengthened day by day. There in the cool of day we shall hear the voice of God walking in the garden speak to us, not in the tones of sorrowful reproof and awful condemnation, as once upon a time, but in such words as fall into our jaded hearts as falls the rain from Heaven upon parched leaf and drooping flower.

This sermon was first preached at Crathie before King George V and Queen Mary on September 14th, 1919, and again in Holy Trinity, St Andrews in July 1920.

Love

Romans XIII 10: Love worketh no ill to his neighbour; therefore love is the fulfilling of the law.

On all sides we are hemmed in by laws. Our physical welfare depends on obedience to them. There are some which we are compelled to follow. Everything we do is controlled by the law of gravity. It is so universal that we are unconscious of its existence. We are free to move as we will, but at the same time we are strictly bound by this law; and when we act as if it did not exist we are at once reminded that it is there, unaltered and unalterable. Yet it is of the utmost use to us if we avail ourselves of its help. There are other laws too which cannot be changed but are of the greatest service to us, if we act in accordance with them, but if we ignore or defy them, we may pay a heavy penalty. On these depend our happiness, our health, even our life itself. A man who declines to be bound by the law of gravity and steps over the edge of a precipice pays at once the price of his temerity. Some laws in nature may at times be defied without immediate harm resulting, but punishment is sure to follow sooner or later if defiance is persisted in.

Then there are countless laws which concern us in the state, in society, even in the Church – laws old and new, written and unwritten. The progress of civilization is not accompanied, as perhaps might have been expected, by any reduction in their number or complexity so far as personal conduct is concerned. If we see with greater clarity than our ancestors the advantages of order we have not fewer laws in consequence but rather a vastly increased number. They are being altered and added to continually. The law factory at Westminster cannot produce them with sufficient speed. More Acts of Parliament are demanded than can be passed. If individual liberty has been increased it is only secured by restrictions which are being enacted in a volume which is amazing and not a little perplexing. Results may justify this feverish activity, but certainly liberty is not to be associated with freedom from laws. Increased liberty may be found in such a multiplication of limitations, but even the most law abiding find difficulty in knowing what they have to observe and obey.

But we have also another system of law – that moral law which is summarily written down in the Ten Commandments, which we speak of as the law of God. This too is fixed for all time and unchangeable, for it is the will of God. He is the giver of this law and He is the judge of it, for you cannot have a law without one who gives it and without one who enforces it. Obedience to it is the act of man's will and he must model his life on it if he is to prosper. Again the penalty for disobedience is not necessarily immediate, but there is a price to be paid sooner or later. Liberty in this case also depends upon law and its observance. Freedom from the evils which are ever ready to enslave a man cannot be obtained if the moral law is broken. There is no force or compulsion to help us in keeping it, though in so far as it is adopted by the laws of the State or the Church there is the element of repression. Obedience to it is voluntary and where it is right obedience to it is to the spirit not the letter of the law. Mankind cannot acquire this for his laws – all he can command is to the letter for he has no legal right to more. The judge has no concern for this higher form of obedience – he cannot inflict punishment because only the letter was observed. The legislator may hope that attention will be paid to the intentions with which the Act has been constructed but he is powerless to extract it. Here is a weakness in all human laws. Penalties can be extracted for neglect of the letter of the law, but man cannot devise punishment for those who neglect the spirit of the law.

Now the law of God given to us in the Ten Commandments is

remarkable for its simplicity and its extreme brevity. In a few words we have a code which covers the ground of duty to God and man. If it were carefully observed not only in the letter but also in the spirit there would be no need for a large part of the law laboriously enacted by man. There is no difficulty in interpretation, no need to call in the services of an expert, or to repair to a court of justice to know what is really meant. A child can understand what is required and what is forbidden. No difficulty is connected with it save in the keeping of it. St John indeed writes in his First Epistle: 'This is the love of God that we keep His Commandment; and His Commandments are not grievous.' Many, feeling such observance most grievous would call in question this statement, but when the divine life is developed and dominant in a man he does truly find them not grievous. If this ideal state were realised there would be no difficulty for mankind here. It is because sin still reigns and the will is not subdued to God's will that grievousness is found or difficulty remains in keeping God's Commandments.

Paul exhorted the Christians in Rome to universal love of others. Let them pay all other debts and be indebted in the matter of love alone. This debt differs from all others in that it increases the more the more it is paid, because the practice of love makes the principle of love deepen and more active. When a man is embued with universal love many difficulties are resolved. The strongest support to a citizen in obeying his country's laws is love – love of country and love of his fellow citizens. However great may be the terrors of the penal code they cannot be compared with love as a means of procuring obedience. For where there is love a man will work no ill to his neighbour – it would be impossible. A life in which all actions are subject to this power is one which cannot contemplate theft, murder, slander, perjury, or covetousness – such actions will be repugnant. Love will dictate the fulfilment of the law and lead to it. The difficulties experienced in obeying any law are vastly lessened when love takes the field. It may not be for the State to exhort men to love one another and their country, but it is certainly the duty of the Church. This is no mere Utopian ideal impossible to carry out – it is intensely practical and many have accepted it and ordered all their actions by it to their own great good and to the profit of others. Get men and women to see the potency of this principle and they will become willing and constant abiders by the law. If it were universally adopted it is clear that the advantage would be incalculable. It is so rarely found that other means to compel obedience have had to be tried. No doubt some will say: 'But you will never make anything of such attempts, it is useless to think of success.' That objection is not warranted by the facts. Love has not been preached in vain. There is a crying need for it in national life today – that its influence is not vastly greater in our social structure is to be laid at the door of the Church which has not preached love with sufficient zeal and continuity. Such controlling power in a man's life makes it natural to strive to obey the Commandments of God. The Commandments cease to be grievous and it is no longer a painful struggle to keep them. But while remaining a duty it is a duty which is not unpleasant to discharge. Our Lord pointed to this when He announced His new Commandment – 'that ye love one another'. There is the true secret of obedience to the moral law. Accept that with all the heart and the rest will follow. You will shrink from all that would harm your neighbour, you will eagerly seize any opportunity of doing him good. Obey the new Commandment and the older ones will present no difficulty, for love is the fulfilment of the law.

Given the will to love – the longing to lighten the burdens and to gladden the lives of others; given the charity which bears, believes, hopes and endures all things, and which envies not and seeks not her own; given the heart set before all things on service to our fellow men and women; and we will obey God. Not in the letter alone will we obey but in spirit as well. Not like the ruler who had kept in the letter all the Commandments given through Moses from his youth up yet lacked the love which would have led him to keep them in spirit. Having this talisman we will love God, the common Father of all, and we will see Him who is Love. We will reverence Him and we will worship no other gods for there will be no idols for us to worship in our hearts or anywhere else.

This sermon was preached in Holy Trinity, St Andrews on September 7th, 1924 and was the last that he wrote.

Light – A Children's Address

Matthew V 14: Ye are the light of the world.

Jesus tells us to let our light shine before men. How can children help to give light to the world? Often we speak of knowledge as light – it removes darkness and guides us. But knowledge alone is not enough. If knowledge was the only way of spreading light children could not do very much, for they are just learners. There are other ways.

One of the great purposes of light is to kill evil. You don't know how much evil light is slaying day by day. There are many weird stories about darkness. What ghosts and hobgoblins inhabit darkness in our story books! But when light comes they all vanish. They cannot live in the sunlight. There is often much truth in fairy tales – darkness and evil go hand in hand. Once there was a window tax, but it was abolished because it was against health. Light is used to deter the thief. Sick people are put not into gloomy rooms but into the sunlight. Light is the enemy of evil.

You must be like light. You can do much to overcome evil. Suppose some children are quarrelling and you approach them cross and ill-tempered, will you do any good? But if you go with a smile and a wish to restore peace you will do good.

You are always doing something to make the world like yourself – bright and happy or gloomy and miserable. A cold firebrand and a burning lamp set off to see what they could find. The firebrand came back disappointed – the whole world was dark. The lamp was full of joy saying: 'Wherever I went there was light.' That was because the lamp gave out light, but the firebrand did not. If you are sweet tempered and fond of peace you will find light wherever you go. You will make others light hearted and glad. If you are petty, jealous, and quarrelsome you will find only darkness. You will cast a black shadow all around.

Yes, children, you have much influence in your homes, in your school, and in your community. Here are some apt lines:

'If I knew the box where the smiles were kept
No matter how large the key
Or strong the bolt, I would try so hard;
'Twould open, I know, for me.
Then over the land and the sea, broadcast,
I'd scatter the smiles to play
That the children's faces might hold them fast
For many and many a day.

If I knew a box that was large enough
To hold all the frowns I meet
I would like to gather them, every one
From nursery, school and street,
Then holding and folding – I'd pack them in
And turning the monster key
I'd hire a giant to drop the box
To the depth of the deep, deep sea.'

Light also creates beauty. It makes the snow lying in the fields and in the streets dazzling white. It makes the frost on the window pane sparkle and glisten. It makes the sea blue and the foam softly bright. It makes the gull's wing pure and the black crow's plumage shine. It gives colour to leaf and flower and fruit. It is so pure and holy that it gives beauty everywhere. It is God's clothing, a part of His being. Therefore it must create beauty. We can help to make others beautiful by being pure ourselves – innocent, spotless, and genuine. 'Be innocent and take heed unto the thing that is right, for that shall bring peace at the last.' Peace and beauty to others as well as to yourselves.

Now a diamond is a perfectly pure stone. When it is cut and light falls on it all sorts of coloured rays shoot out – red, yellow, blue, green, orange, violet. There is a good deal of diamond all around us ready to burst into beauty if light falls on it. Often there is a rough diamond, perhaps cut on one side only – let us direct our light towards it so that it may become resplendent. A little light will do it and then it will brighten others. But we can only reflect light. Let us direct our attention to the source.

And light makes us glad. It causes the birds to sing in the spring and the smile to cover the face of nature in the summer morning. So we must, you must, be like the light and help to make others glad. Make that a definite aim day by day.

How unselfish the light is! It gains nothing for itself. So we must be unselfish – willing to give up something for the sake of others – just to make them glad.

Christ was and is the Light of the world. He came to make us kind, pure and unselfish.

This children's address was first delivered in Holy Trinity, St Andrews on February 2nd, 1902, and later in St Katharine's School, St Andrews in November 1921.